Lab Manual for MCSE Guide to
Microsoft® Windows® Server 2003 Active Directory

Michael Aubert

THOMSON
COURSE TECHNOLOGY

Australia • Canada • Mexico • Singapore • Spain • United Kingdom • United States

THOMSON
TM
COURSE TECHNOLOGY

Lab Manual for MCSE Guide to a Microsoft Windows Server 2003 Active Directory

by Michael Aubert

Managing Editor:
Will Pitkin III

Product Manager:
Nick Lombardi

Production Editor:
Brooke Booth

Developmental Editor:
Ralph E. Moore

Technical Edit/Quality Assurance:
Marianne Snow
Chris Scriver
Shawn Day

Associate Product Manager:
Mirella Misiaszek
David Rivera

Editorial Assistant:
Amanda Piantedosi

Senior Manufacturing Coordinator:
Trevor Kallop

Senior Marketing Manager:
Jason Sakos

Text Designer:
GEX Publishing Services

Compositor:
GEX Publishing Services

Cover Design:
Steve Deschene

TABLE OF
Contents

CHAPTER 3

Active Directory Design Philosophy   49

CHAPTER 4

Active Directory Architecture   63

CHAPTER 5

Active Directory Logical Design   **85**

CHAPTER 6

Active Directory Physical Design   **103**

CHAPTER 7

CHAPTER 8

CHAPTER 9

Active Directory Authentication and Security   **155**

CHAPTER 10

Managing Users, Groups, Computers, and Resources   **173**

CHAPTER 11

Group Policy for Corporate Policy **193**

CHAPTER 12

Deploying and Managing Software with Group Policy   **211**

Introduction

The objective of this lab manual is to assist you in preparing for the 70-294 exam, Planning, Implementing, and Maintaining a Microsoft Windows Server 2003 Active Directory Infrastructure, as well as a career in Microsoft network implementation and management, using Microsoft's enterprise-level directory service, Active Directory. This text is designed to be used in conjunction with *MCSE Guide to Microsoft Windows Server 2003 Active Directory* (ISBN: 0-619-13017-2), and it should be noted that many of the labs rely upon activities from the *MCSE Guide* being completed first. Additionally, it is important that you complete the lab manual activities for each chapter after the activities in the *MCSE Guide*, but before progressing on to the next chapter of the *MCSE Guide*. For example, after completing activities in Chapter 1 of the *MCSE Guide*, you should then complete the activities in Chapter 1 of this lab manual. Once you have completed the activities in Chapter 1 of both texts, you can then complete the activities in Chapter 2 of the *MCSE Guide*, followed by Chapter 2 of this lab manual. If activities are not completed in this order, students may get different results from the labs. Although this manual is written to be used in a classroom lab environment, it also may be used for self-study on a home network.

Features

In order to ensure a successful experience for instructors and students alike, this book includes the following features:

- **Lab Objectives** – The goal of each lab is clearly stated at the beginning.

- **Materials Required** – Every lab includes information on hardware, software, and other materials that you will need to complete the lab.

- **Estimated Completion Time** – Every lab has an estimated completion time, so that you can plan your activities more accurately.

- **Activity Background** – Activity Background information provides important details and prepares students for the activity that follows.

- **Activity Sections** – Labs are presented in manageable sections and include figures to reinforce learning.

- **Step-by-Step Instructions** – Steps provide practice, which enhances technical proficiency.

- **Microsoft Windows Server 2003 MCSE Certification Objectives** – For each lab, the relevant objectives from MCSE Exam #70-294 are listed.

- **Review Questions** – Review reinforces concepts presented in the lab.

Hardware Requirements

All hardware in the computer should be listed on the Hardware Compatibility List available at *www.microsoft.com*.

Operating System	Microsoft Windows Server 2003
CPU	Pentium III 550 or higher
Memory	128 MB RAM (256 MB RAM recommended)
Disk Space	Minimum of two 4-GB partitions (C and D), with at least 1 GB of free space left on the drive
Drives	CD-ROM Floppy Disk
Networking	All lab computers should be networked. Students will work in pairs for some lab exercises. A connection to the Internet via some sort of NAT or Proxy server is assumed.

Software Requirements

The following software is needed for proper setup of the labs:

- Microsoft Windows Server 2003, Enterprise Edition or Standard Edition

Setup Procedure

1. Install Windows Server 2003 onto drive C: of the instructor and student servers. The following specific parameters should be configured on individual servers during the installation process:

Parameter	Setting
Disk Partitioning	Create two 4-GB NTFS partitions during the installation process, C and D. Ensure that at least 1 GB of free space is left on the hard disk for student exercises.
Computer Names	Instructor (first server), ServerXX (subsequent student servers)
Administrator Password	Password01
Components	Default Settings
Network Adapter	IP Address: 192.168.1.X. The instructor computer should be allocated a unique IP address on the same subnet as client computers. The suggested IP address for the Instructor machine is 192.168.1.100.
	Subnet Mask: 255.255.255.0
	DNS: The IP address of the Instructor computer.
	Default Gateway: The IP address for the classroom default gateway.
	If the Instructor computer will be used to provide Internet access via ICS or NAT, it will require a second network adapter card or modem.
Workgroup Name	Workgroup

In the table above, "X" or "XX" should represent a unique number to be assigned to each student. For example, student "1" would be assigned a computer name of Server01 and an IP address of 192.168.1.1.

2. Once the installation process is complete, use Device Manager to ensure that all devices are functioning correctly. In some cases, it may be necessary to download and install additional drivers for devices listed with a yellow question mark icon.

3. Create a new folder named Source on drive D: of all classroom servers. Copy the entire contents of the Windows Server 2003 CD to this folder on all servers.

4. Create a new folder named Shared on drive D: of the Instructor computer only. Share this folder using the shared folder name Shared, and ensure that the Everyone group is granted the Full Control shared folder permission. This folder will be used to store any supplemental files that may need to be made available to students during the course.

5. Run dcpromo.exe on the Instructor computer to install Active Directory and DNS. Name the new domain (the first in a new forest) supercorp.net, ensure that both nonsecure and secure dynamic updates are allowed, and accept all other default options.

6. On the Instructor computer's DNS server, create a reverse lookup zone for 192.168.1.X and accept all the default options.

7. Student servers should remain member servers in the workgroup named Workgroup. The Active Directory structure in the classroom once this is complete is illustrated in the following figure.

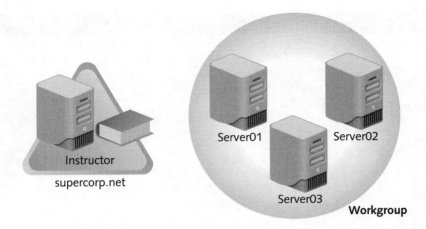

8. On each student server, use the Computer Management console to add a user account named Admin*XX*, where *XX* corresponds to the server number assigned to each server. The password associated with this account should be Password01. Also be sure to set up the account so that the password never expires. This account should be added to the Administrators group on the local server.

NOTE   Many of the labs rely upon activities from the *MCSE Guide to Microsoft Windows Server 2003 Active Directory* (ISBN: 0-619-13017-2) being completed first. Without completing those activities first, students may get different results from the labs. For more details, see the introduction earlier in this text.

ACKNOWLEDGMENTS

This text is the product of the talents of many individuals. First, I'd like to thank my colleague, Dan DiNicolo, for all his hard work in developing the content for this text. I also wish to thank the staff at Course Technology for an enjoyable experience writing a networking textbook on Windows Server 2003. More specifically, I wish to thank my Project Manager, Nick Lombardi, for his patience and insight; my Production Editor, Brooke Booth, for her ability to keep everyone on track; as well as my Developmental Editor, Ralph Moore, for his cheerfulness and wit while working this text into its current state. As well, I wish to thank Moirag Haddad at Digital Content Factory for her advice and guidance.

Thanks also to the reviewers, Patty Gillilan, Norwood Nutting, and Ron Houle, whose insightful comments were of invaluable assistance in the creation of this text.

Michael Aubert
mike@2000trainers.com

Acknowledgment

INTRODUCTION TO ACTIVE DIRECTORY

Labs included in this chapter:

♦ Lab 1.1 Identifying the primary tools used to manage Active Directory

♦ Lab 1.2 Connecting to a Server with Remote Desktop

♦ Lab 1.3 Searching Active Directory

♦ Lab 1.4 Using Saved Queries

♦ Lab 1.5 Browsing Active Directory using the Command Prompt

♦ Lab 1.6 Using Help and Support to Learn About Active Directory

Microsoft MCSE Exam #70-294 Objectives	
Objective	Lab
Manage an Active Directory forest and domain structure.	1.1, 1.2, 1.3, 1.4, 1.5
Manage an Active Directory site.	1.1, 1.2
Troubleshoot Active Directory.	1.6

LAB 1.1 IDENTIFYING THE PRIMARY TOOLS USED TO MANAGE ACTIVE DIRECTORY

Objectives

The goal of this lab is to gain familiarity with the primary tools you can use to manage Active Directory.

Materials Required

This lab will require the following:

■ A Windows Server 2003 setup, as directed at the front of this lab manual

Estimated completion time: **15 minutes**

Activity Background

In order to successfully configure Active Directory, you must first be aware of the tools available. When a Windows Server 2003 system is promoted to a domain controller, three additional consoles are available from the Administrative Tools menu: Active Directory Domains and Trusts, Active Directory Sites and Services, and Active Directory Users and Computers. This lab shows you how to access these three consoles and describes what each is used for.

ACTIVITY

Activity

1. If necessary, start your server and log on using the **AdminXX** account in the **CHILDXX** domain (where *XX* is the number of your server) using the password **Password01**.

2. Click **Start**, point to **Administrative Tools**, and then click **Active Directory Domains and Trusts**. The Active Directory Domains and Trusts management console appears, as shown in Figure 1-1. Using this console, you can manage the domains that make up a forest and the trust relationships for each domain.

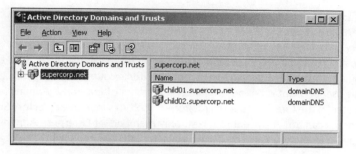

Figure 1-1   Active Directory Domains and Trusts

3. With supercorp.net selected in the left tree pane, right–click **childXX.supercorp.net** (where *XX* is the number of your server) in the right details pane and then click **Properties**.

4. In the child*XX*.supercorp.net Properties window, note the tabs available and the information found on each.

5. Once you have noted the information available, click **Cancel** to close the Properties window.

6. Close the Active Directory Domains and Trusts console.

7. Click **Start**, point to **Administrative Tools**, and then click **Active Directory Sites and Services**. The Active Directory Sites and Services management console appears, as shown in Figure 1-2. Using this console, you can manage sites, site links, subnets, and replication across the entire forest.

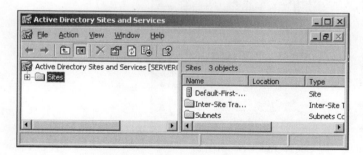

Figure 1-2   Active Directory Sites and Services

8. In the left tree pane, expand the **Sites** node, the **Default–First–Site–Name** site node, and the **Servers** node.

9. In the left tree pane, click **SERVERXX** (where *XX* is the number of your server) under the Servers node.

10. In the right details pane, right-click the **NTDS Settings** object and click **Properties**.

11. In the NTDS Settings Properties window, note the tabs available and the information found on each.

TIP
Most of the options in Active Directory Sites and Services will be disabled because you are logged on using a domain administrator account from your child domain. This user account is not automatically a member of Enterprise Admins (a group located in the forest root domain). Because settings in Active Directory Sites and Services can affect the entire forest, only members of Enterprise Admins are allowed to modify these configuration settings.

12. Once you have noted the information available, click **Cancel** to close the Properties window.

13. Close the Active Directory Sites and Services console.

14. Click **Start**, point to **Administrative Tools**, and then click **Active Directory Users and Computers**. The Active Directory Users and Computers management console appears. Using this console you can manage the objects—such as user accounts, computer accounts, groups, and published printers—that are contained within an Active Directory domain.

15. In the left tree pane, double-click **childXX.supercorp.net** (where *XX* is the number of your server) to expand the node and reveal its details in the right pane, as shown in Figure 1-3.

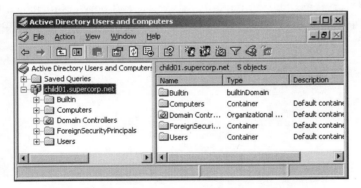

Figure 1-3   Active Directory Users and Computers

16. Note the different containers and the types of objects located in each container underneath child*XX*.supercorp.net by default. You can use the Type column in the right details pane to identify the type of object.

17. Close the Active Directory Users and Computers console.

18. Log off your server if you do not intend to immediately continue to the next project. Otherwise, stay logged on.

Certification O~~~

[handwritten note: 1 B 2 C 3 Domains & Trusts 4 Sites & Services 5 B]

Objectives for M~~~ ~~~ng, Implementing, and Maintaining a Microsoft Windo~~~ Infrastructure:

- Manage ~~~ ~~~main structure.

- Manage a~~~

REVIEW QUESTIONS

1. What too~~~ a server is acting as a Global Catalog?

    a. Active ~~~

    b. Active ~~~

    c. Active ~~~ and Computers

    d. Active Directory Replication and Configuration

2. In Active Directory Users and Computers, where is the computer account for your domain controller SERVERXX located by default?

    a. Builtin

    b. Computers

    c. Domain Controllers

    d. Users

3. You can use _____ to manage the trust relationships between domains.

4. You can use _____ to manage replication between domain controllers.

5. When attempting to modify the Active Directory physical structure, you receive an error message informing you that access has been denied. Additionally, many of the options are grayed out and can't be modified. What is the most likely reason?

    a. Your account is not a member of Forest Admins.

    b. Your account is not a member of Enterprise Admins.

    c. Your account is not a member of System Admins.

    d. Your account is not a member of Structure Admins.

Lab 1.2 Connecting to a Server with Remote Desktop

Objectives

The goal of this lab is to learn how to use Remote Desktop to make a connection to another server.

Materials Required

This lab will require the following:

- A Windows Server 2003 setup, as directed at the front of this lab manual

Estimated completion time: **15 minutes**

Activity Background

You use Remote Desktop to manage a remote computer running Windows Server 2003 or Windows XP Professional as if you were physically sitting in front of the computer. This lab will show you how to enable remote desktop on a Windows Server 2003 system and explore the different tools available to establish a remote desktop connection. Keep in mind that the tools used to access computers running Remote Desktop can also be used to access Windows 2000 servers running Terminal Services.

ACTIVITY

Activity

1. If necessary, start your server and log on using the **AdminXX** account in the **CHILDXX** domain (where *XX* is the number of your server) using the password **Password01**.

2. Click **Start**, point to **Control Panel**, and then click **System**.

3. Click the **Remote** tab.

4. In the Remote Desktop section, check the **Allow users to connect remotely to this computer** check box, as shown in Figure 1-4. A message box appears informing you that accounts used to establish remote sessions must have a password.

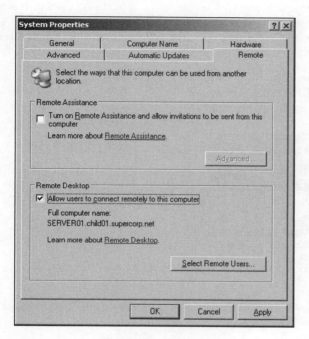

Figure 1-4   Enabling Remote Desktop

5. Click **OK**.

6. Click **Select Remote Users**.

7. Confirm that no additional users or groups are displayed in the list of users who can connect to the computer remotely. Members of the Administrators group can connect to the computer remotely even if their user account is not listed. Click **OK**.

8. In the System Properties window, click **OK** to save the changes made. Remote Desktop is now enabled.

You will need to wait for your partner to complete the previous steps on his or her server before continuing.

NOTE

9. There are two tools included with Windows Server 2003 that you can use to establish remote sessions. The first tool, Remote Desktop Connection, is designed to make a single connection at a time, although you can establish multiple connections to the same or multiple servers by running multiple instances of the Remote Desktop Connection application. To run Remote Desktop Connection, click **Start**, point to **All Programs**, point to **Accessories**, point to **Communications**, and then click **Remote Desktop Connection**.

10. In the Computer drop-down combo box, type **SERVERXX.childXX.supercorp.net** (where *XX* is the number of your partner's server) as shown in Figure 1-5.

Figure 1-5   Using Remote Desktop Connection to connect to another computer

11. Click the **Options >>** button to display additional connection options. Note the tabs available and the types of options each contains.

12. Once you have noted the options available, click **Connect**.

13. Log on to the remote computer using the **AdminXX** account in the **CHILDXX** domain (where *XX* is the number of your partner's server) using the password **Password01**. The desktop of the remote server appears.

14. Click **Start** and then click **Log Off**.

15. In the Log Off Windows message box, click **Log Off**. The desktop of your local server reappears.

TIP   Logging off a remote session and disconnecting from a remote session are not the same thing. When you log off from a remote session, your applications are closed, the session is ended, and any resources, such as memory, are freed. In contrast, when you disconnect from a remote session by closing Remote Desktop Connection or Remote Desktops without first logging off of the remote session, the remote session and applications continue to run on the remote computer. When you reconnect to the server, the same remote session is reestablished.

16. Managing many servers and workstations using Remote Desktop Connection can be difficult. You can use an additional application, Remote Desktops, to manage many computers remotely at a single time. To start Remote Desktops, click **Start**, select **Administrative Tools**, and then click **Remote Desktops**.

17. In the left tree pane, right–click Remote Desktops and click **Add new connection**.

18. In the Server name or IP address text box, type **SERVER*XX*.child*XX*.supercorp.net** (where *XX* is the number of your partner's server).

19. In the Connection name text box, remove the automatically generated name and type **SERVER*XX*** (where *XX* is the number of your partner's server) and then click **OK**.

20. In the left tree pane, expand the **Remote Desktops** node and then click **SERVER*XX*** (where *XX* is the number of your partner's server). You can now log on to the remote computer as shown in Figure 1-6.

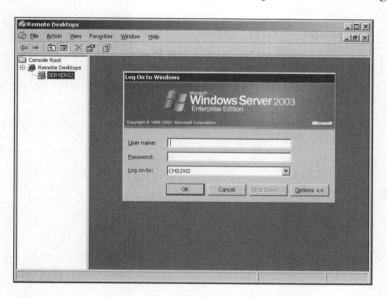

Figure 1-6   Using Remote Desktops to connect to another computer

21. Close the Remote Desktops console without logging on to the remote server. When prompted if you would like to save the console, click **No**.

22. Log off your server if you do not intend to immediately continue to the next project. Otherwise, stay logged on.

Certification Objectives

Objectives for Microsoft Exam #70-294: Planning, Implementing, and Maintaining a Microsoft Windows Server 2003 Active Directory Infrastructure:

- Manage an Active Directory forest and domain structure.

- Manage an Active Directory site.

REVIEW QUESTIONS

Handwritten note overlaying text:
1. Administrators
2. No Remote Desktops
3. A Remote Desktop
4. Disconnect Connection
5. False True if
   (Running) Terminal Services

1. When Remote D _____ the _____ group are automatically allc

2. You can use _____ many servers and workstations simultaneously.

3. When creating a _____ ich application allows you to specify logon cre _____ tablished?

   a. Remote Desk

   b. Remote Desk

   c. Secure Deskt

   d. Both Remot _____ ote Desktops

4. You can _____ ich will allow the applications you have opened to continue to run.

5. You can establish a remote desktop connection to a computer running Windows 2000 Professional. True or False?

LAB 1.3 SEARCHING ACTIVE DIRECTORY

Objectives

The goal of this lab is to learn how an end user can search Active Directory to locate objects.

Materials Required

This lab will require the following:

- A Windows Server 2003 setup, as directed at the front of this lab manual

Estimated completion time: **10 minutes**

Activity Background

While an administrator typically has access to Active Directory Users and Computers, it is not a tool that is designed for end users of the network. To allow end users access to the information stored in Active Directory, such as lists of shared printers or folders, Windows 2000, Windows XP, and Windows Server 2003 all provide similar search capabilities integrated with the operating system. In this lab you will learn how to use the integrated search capabilities of Windows Server 2003 to locate all published printers in the directory.

Activity

1. If necessary, start your server and log on using the **AdminXX** account in the **CHILDXX** domain (where *XX* is the number of your server) using the password **Password01**.

2. Click **Start** and then click **Search**.

3. In the left pane, click **Other search options**. You may need to scroll down or expand the Search Results window in order to see Other search options.

4. In the left pane under What do you want to search for?, click **Printers, computers, or people**. The What are you looking for? screen appears in the left pane, as shown in Figure 1-7.

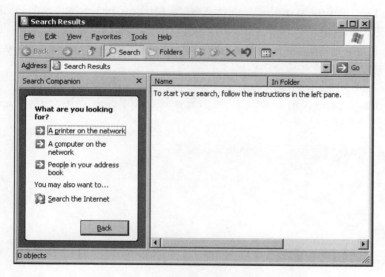

Figure 1-7   What are you looking for? screen

5. Click **A printer on the network**. The Find Printers window appears. On the Printers and Features tab, you can specify the most common attributes used to search for printers. On the Advanced tab, you can specify additional attributes on which you want to search.

TIP

The Find Printers window supports the asterisk (*) wildcard, which represents zero or more characters. For example, you can search for *Laser* in the Model attribute to find all printers that have the word Laser anywhere in the model attribute.

6. Leave all text boxes and options blank, and then click **Find Now** to find all printers in the directory. If your instructor has made a printer available on the network and published it in Active Directory, it will appear in the lower half of the Find Printers window.

Only printers that have been published in Active Directory are searchable. Computers running Windows Server 2003, Windows XP Professional, or Windows 2000 will automatically publish any printers they share.

7. Close the Find Printers window.

8. In the Search Results window, click **People in your address book**.

9. In the Find People window, select **Active Directory** in the Look in drop-down list box.

10. In the Name text box, type **AdminXX** (where *XX* is the number of your server) and click **Find Now**.

11. When the results are displayed, double-click **AdminXX** in the results list. The properties for the Admin*XX* user account are displayed as shown in Figure 1-8. Note the tabs available.

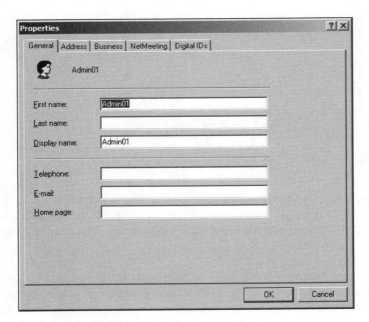

Figure 1-8   Admin*XX* user account properties

12. Click **OK**.

13. Close the Find People window.

14. Close the Search Results window.

15. Log off your server if you do not intend to immediately continue to the next project. Otherwise, stay logged on.

Certification Objectives

Objectives for Microsoft Exam ~~...~~ ~~...~~ ~~...~~ ~~...~~ ting, and Maintaining a Microsoft Windows Server 200~~...~~

- Manage an Active Dire~~...~~

REVIEW QUESTIONS

1. You can use the _____ ~~...~~ rs in Active Directory.

2. You can use the _____ ~~...~~ Active Directory.

3. To find all printers who ~~...~~ s and ends with Letter, which of the following ~~...~~

   a. Sales*Letter

   b. *Sales*Letter

   c. Sales*Letter*

   d. *Sales*Letter*

4. A printer must be _____ in Active Directory in order for users to search for the printer.

5. Which of the following operating systems does not publish printers automatically?

   a. Windows Server 2003

   b. Windows XP Professional

   c. Windows 2000 Professional

   d. Windows 98 Second Edition

[Handwritten note: 1. Search Printers 2. Search People 3. A 4 Published 5 D]

LAB 1.4 USING SAVED QUERIES

Objectives

The goal of this lab is to learn how to create Saved Queries in Active Directory Users and Computers.

Materials Required

This lab will require the following:

- A Windows Server 2003 setup, as directed at the front of this lab manual

---

Estimated completion time: **10 minutes**

Activity Background

Although the search feature located on the Start menu allows end users to search for objects in the directory, it is very limited. Administrators can use a new feature in Active Directory named Saved Queries to build complex search queries that can be saved and used again. This lab will show you how to create a saved query that lists all users who have passwords that never expire (which means the user is never forced to change their password).

Activity

1. If necessary, start your server and log on using the **AdminXX** account in the **CHILDXX** domain (where *XX* is the number of your server) using the password **Password01**.

2. Click **Start**, point to **Administrative Tools**, and then click **Active Directory Users and Computers**.

3. Right-click **Saved Queries** in the left tree pane, select **New**, and then click **Query**.

If you are performing a one-time search, you can right-click a container in Active Directory Users and Computers and click Find... instead of creating a Saved Query. The difference between Saved Queries and the Find feature is that Find does not save queries for reuse later. Additionally, you can use Find to search the entire forest at once, whereas Saved Queries are limited to a single domain.

4. In the New Query window, type **Passwords Never Expire** in the Name text box.

5. In the Description text box, type **User accounts whose passwords will never expire**.

6. Leave the Query root as the default, and ensure that the **Include subcontainers** check box is checked so that the search will include the root of the domain and all of its subcontainers.

7. Click the **Define Query** button.

8. In the Find Common Queries window, check the **Non expiring passwords** check box and click **OK**. The Query string text box in the New Query window updates to show the LDAP query as shown in Figure 1-9.

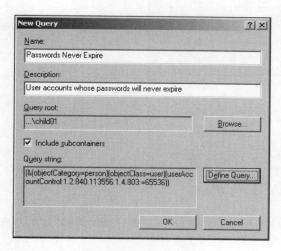

Figure 1-9   New Query window

9. Click **OK**. The results of the new query should now be displayed in the right pane. If the results are not automatically displayed on your server, expand the **Saved Queries** folder in the left tree pane and then click **Passwords Never Expire**.

10. To modify the query to exclude the Guest account, right-click the query **Passwords Never Expire** in the left tree pane and click **Edit**.

11. Click the **Define Query** button.

12. In the Name drop-down list box, select **Is not**. Note the other options available.

13. In the Name text box, type **Guest**.

14. Click **OK** in the Find Common Queries window.

15. Click **OK** in the Edit Query window.

16. To refresh the query results, right-click **Passwords Never Expire** in the left tree pane and click **Refresh**. Figure 1-10 shows the updated query results.

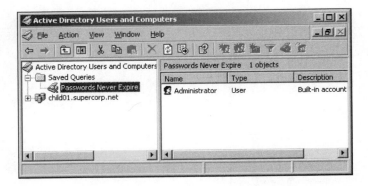

Figure 1-10   Passwords Never Expire query results

 Depending on the user accounts created on your server, you may have different or additional user accounts that are not shown in Figure 1-10.

17. Close Active Directory Users and Computers.

18. Log off your server if you do not intend to immediately continue to the next project. Otherwise, stay logged on.

Certification Objectives

Objectives for Microsoft Exam #70-294: Planning, ~~Implementing, and Maintaining~~ a Microsoft Windows Server 2003 Active Directory In~~frastructure~~

- Manage an Active Directory forest and domain structure.

REVIEW QUESTIONS

1. You can use _____ to create queries that are reusable.

2. You can use _____ to create a query for one-time use.

3. When you are defining the name of a user account in a query, which of the following is not a valid option?

   a. Starts With

   b. Ends With

   c. Contains

   d. Has a value

4. After you edit a saved query, the results do not update. What must you do to update the results?

   a. Right-click the query and click Rerun.

   b. Right-click the query and click Refresh.

   c. Right-click the query and click Rename.

   d. Right-click the query and click Execute.

5. When defining a saved query, the Query root specifies which of the following?

   a. Which tree you would like to search.

   b. Which root you would like to search.

   c. Which container you would like to search.

   d. Which forest you would like to search.

LAB 1.5 BROWSING ACTIVE DIRECTORY USING THE COMMAND PROMPT

Objectives

The goal of this lab is to gain familiarity with the command line tools that you can use to view and query Active Directory.

Materials Required

This lab will require the following:

- A Windows Server 2003 setup, as directed at the front of this lab manual

Estimated completion time: **10 minutes**

Activity Background

The Active Directory Users and Computers console is used to perform most everyday administration of Active Directory. However, in Windows Server 2003, the following new command-line tools have been introduced for managing and viewing the directory: dsadd, dsget, dsmod, dsmove, dsquery, and dsrm. These new command-line tools support several options and advanced features. In this lab you will be introduced to two of these tools, dsget and dsquery. Keep in mind that you can get help on any of these commands by typing one of the commands at a prompt followed by /? (for example, *dsget /?*) or by searching Help and Support.

Activity

1. If necessary, start your server and log on using the **AdminXX** account in the **CHILDXX** domain (where *XX* is the number of your server) using the password **Password01**.

2. Click **Start** and then click **Command Prompt**.

3. At the command prompt, type **dsquery user "CN=Users,DC=childXX,DC=supercorp,DC=net"** (where *XX* is the number of your server) and press **Enter**. The user accounts in the Users container of the child*XX*.supercorp.net domain are displayed, as shown in Figure 1-11.

You can type dsquery /? and press enter to display the dsquery command-line tool help. For additional information on using dsquery to query user objects, type dsquery user /? and press Enter.

Figure 1-11   User accounts in the Users container

Depending on the user accounts created on your server, you may have different or additional user accounts that are not shown in Figure 1-11.

4. To display the groups of which the Administrator is a member, type **dsget user "CN=Administrator,CN=Users,DC=child*XX*,DC=supercorp,DC=net" –memberOf** (where *XX* is the number of your server) and press **Enter**. The groups the Administrator account is a member of are displayed as shown in Figure 1-12.

TIP You can type dsget /? and press enter to display the dsget command-line tool help. For additional information on using dsget to query user objects, type dsget user /? and press Enter.

Figure 1-12   Groups the Administrator account is a member of

5. To close the Command Prompt window, type **Exit** and press **Enter**.

6. Log off your server after finishing the review questions if you do not intend to immediately continue to the next project. Otherwise, stay logged on.

Certification Objectives

Objectives for Microsoft Exam #70-294: Planning, Implementing, and Maintaining a Microsoft Windows Server 2003 Active Directory Infrastructure:

■ Manage an Active Directory forest and domain structure.

REVIEW QUESTIONS

1. You can use the _____ parameter of the *dsget user* command to display a user's e-mail address.

2. You can use the *dsget* _____ command to view the attributes of an organizational unit.

3. To view help on using dsquery with group objects, type _____ at the command prompt.

4. Which of the following commands would display all user account objects in the Sales organizational unit in the domain.com domain?

   a. dsquery user "OU=Sales,DC=domain,DC=com"

   b. dsquery user "CN=Sales,DC=domain,DC=com"

   c. dsget user "OU=Sales,DC=domain,DC=com"

   d. dsget user "CN=Sales,DC=domain,DC=com"

5. Which of the following commands can you use to find all user accounts that have an RDN that begins with "A"?

   a. dsquery user –rdn "A"

   b. dsquery user –rdn "A*"

   c. dsquery user –name "A"

   d. dsquery user –name "A*"

LAB 1.6 USING HELP AND SUPPORT TO LEARN ABOUT ACTIVE DIRECTORY

Objectives

The goal of this lab is to view a checklist of steps to perform before you create an additional domain controller in an existing domain and to use Help and Support as a tool to find out more information regarding Active Directory.

Materials Required

This lab will require the following:

- A Windows Server 2003 setup, as directed at the front of this lab manual

Estimated completion time: **15 minutes**

Activity Background

One of the most important responsibilities of an administrator is to find information. Fortunately, Windows Server 2003 provides built-in support that can give you detailed information on a wide range of topics. In this lab you will be introduced to the Windows Server 2003 Help and Support Center.

ACTIVITY

Activity

1. If necessary, start your server and log on using the **AdminXX** account in the **CHILDXX** domain (where *XX* is the number of your server) using the password **Password01**.

2. Click **Start** and then click **Help and Support**.

3. Under Help Contents, click **Active Directory**. The main Active Directory support screen appears, as shown in Figure 1-13.

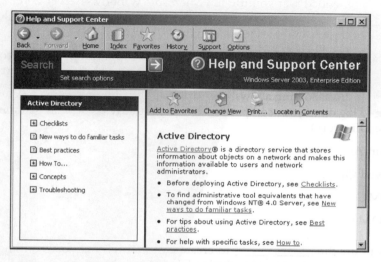

Figure 1-13   Active Directory Help and Support

4. In the right pane, click the **Checklists** hyperlink and then click the **Checklist: Creating an additional domain controller in an existing domain** hyperlink.

5. Make a note (a few words summarizing each step is sufficient) of the steps you should perform before you promote a domain controller in an existing domain.

6. Click the **Back** button to return to the list of checklists.

7. Click the **Back** button to return to the main Active Directory help screen.

8. Familiarize yourself with the type of information available to you through Help and Support on Active Directory. The Review Questions that follow will be based upon information that you can find here.

9. Log off your server after finishing the review questions.

Certification Objectives

Objectives for Microsoft Exam #70-294: Planning, Implementing, and Maintaining a Microsoft Windows Server 2003 Active Directory Infrastructure:

- Troubleshoot Active Directory.

REVIEW QUESTIONS

1. It is recommended that you use the Microsoft Windows Server 2003 _____ as a resource when deploying domain controllers. (Deploying Active Directory > Deployment resources)

2. You can use the _____ Active Directory support tool resource to analyze the state of domain controllers. (Resources > Active Directory support tools)

3. Which of the fol_____ _____ you to accomplish administrative tasks without having t_____ _____ er with administrative credentials? (Administering

   c.

   d.

4. You _____ _____ e custom tools that focus on single managem_____ _____ irectory > Managing Active Directory from _____

5. _____ _____ t provides a simple, powerful, object-oriented _____ _____ sources > Programming interfaces)

2

NAME RESOLUTION AND DNS

Labs included in this chapter:

- ◆ Lab 2.1 Using NBTSTAT and IPCONFIG
- ◆ Lab 2.2 Refreshing and Verifying Domain Controller DNS Records
- ◆ Lab 2.3 Creating a Primary and Secondary Forward Lookup Zone
- ◆ Lab 2.4 Creating a Primary Reverse Lookup Zone
- ◆ Lab 2.5 Adding Records to a DNS Zone
- ◆ Lab 2.6 Modifying DNS Zone Settings

Microsoft MCSE Exam #70-294 Objectives	
Objective	Lab
Implement an Active Directory directory service forest and domain structure.	2.3, 2.4, 2.5
Manage an Active Directory forest and domain structure.	2.5, 2.6
Troubleshoot Active Directory.	2.1, 2.2

LAB 2.1 USING NBTSTAT AND IPCONFIG

Objectives

The goal of this lab is to gain familiarity with the tools used to manage the NetBIOS and DNS name resolution caches and record registration.

Materials Required

This lab will require the following:

- A Windows Server 2003 setup, as directed at the front of this lab manual

Estimated completion time: **10 minutes**

Activity Background

Name resolution is one of the most important services on a network. If name resolution is improperly configured, users' network access may be very slow or not work at all. To help an administrator troubleshoot name resolution issues, Windows Server 2003 provides several tools that for managing both DNS and NetBIOS name resolution on a system. In this lab you will learn about the NBTSTAT and IPCONFIG utilities.

Activity

1. If necessary, start your server and log on using the **AdminXX** account in the **CHILDXX** domain (where *XX* is the number of your server) using the password **Password01**.

2. Click **Start** and then click **Command Prompt**.

3. In the Command Prompt window, type **NBTSTAT –c** and press **Enter**. The computer's NetBIOS name cache is displayed. Unless you have recently accessed another computer over the network using a NetBIOS name, or have entries in the lmhost file (discussed shortly), the cache will be empty.

For help on using the NBTSTAT command, type NBTSTAT without any parameters and press Enter.

PING is a utility that you can use to test the TCP/IP connectivity between two computers. When pinging another system, a data packet is sent from your computer and is addressed to the target computer. If the target computer receives the ping packet, the target computer sends a reply to the computer that sent the data packet.

2

4. Type **PING SERVERXX** (where *XX* is the number of your partner's server) and press Enter. Your server must resolve the name of your partner's server using NetBIOS name resolution, because it will be unable to resolve the name using DNS.

NOTE

The reason DNS name resolution fails is because only a host name is provided and not an FQDN. When your server attempts to resolve the name, it must append a DNS suffix to the host name. By default, the primary DNS suffix of your server—child*XX*.supercorp.net (where *XX* is the number of your server)—is first appended. If that FQDN fails to be resolved when submitted to DNS for resolution, one label of the DNS name is removed. The request is resubmitted to the DNS until there are only two labels left in the suffix. Because neither SERVERZZ.child*XX*.supercorp.net nor SERVERZZ.supercorp.net (where *XX* is the number of your server and *ZZ* is the number of your partner's server) will resolve to a valid FQDN, DNS name resolution fails.

5. Type **NBTSTAT –c** and press **Enter**. The computer's NetBIOS name cache is displayed as shown in Figure 2-1.

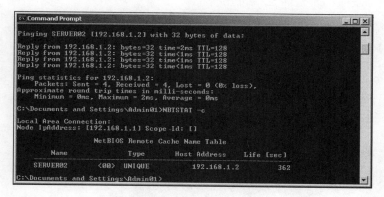

Figure 2-1   NetBIOS name cache

6. When troubleshooting name resolution issues, it may become necessary to clear the NetBIOS name cache. To clear the cache, type **NBTSTAT –R** and press **Enter**.

TIP

You can use the lmhosts file located in %systemroot%\system32\drivers\etc to map IP addresses to NetBIOS names manually. The file is named lmhosts.sam by default, so you will need to remove the .sam extension, or create a new file named lmhosts without an extension.

7. Type **NBTSTAT –c** and press **Enter** to view the cleared NetBIOS name cache.

8. When troubleshooting name resolution issues, it may also become necessary to clear the NetBIOS name cache and have a computer reregister its records in WINS. To clear the cache and reregister WINS records, type **NBTSTAT -RR** and press **Enter**.

9. While NBTSTAT is used to manage NetBIOS name resolution, you use IPCONFIG to manage the DNS resolver cache. To view the DNS name cache, type **IPCONFIG /displaydns** and press **Enter**. The computer's DNS cache is displayed. Unless you have recently accessed another computer over the network using a DNS name, the only resolved names in the cache are for the local computer.

 For help on using the IPCONFIG command, type IPCONFIG /? and press Enter.

 You can use the host name localhost and the IP address 127.0.0.1, which is referred to as the "loopback" address, for testing that the TCP/IP protocol is installed correctly on your computer.

10. Type **PING SERVER*XX*.child*XX*.supercorp.net** (where *XX* is the number of your partner's server) and press **Enter**. Your server will use DNS name resolution to resolve the FQDN.

11. Type **IPCONFIG /displaydns** and press **Enter**. The computer's DNS resolver cache is displayed as shown in Figure 2-2.

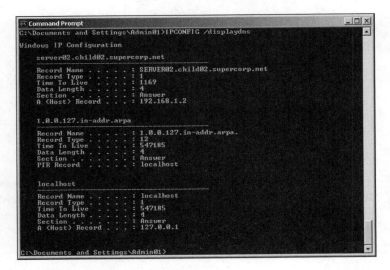

Figure 2-2   DNS resolver cache

12. When troubleshooting name resolution issues, it may sometimes be necessary to clear the DNS resolver cache. To clear the DNS resolver cache, type **IPCONFIG /flushdns** and press **Enter**.

13. Type **IPCONFIG /displaydns** and press **Enter** to view the cleared DNS resolver cache. (Note that records contained in the hosts file still appear.)

> **TIP** You can use the hosts file located in %systemroot%\system32\drivers\etc to map IP addresses to host names manually. By default, an entry that maps 127.0.0.1 to localhost exists in the hosts file.

14. When troubleshooting name resolution issues, it may become necessary to have a computer reregister its records in DNS. To reregister DNS records, type **IPCONFIG /registerdns** and press **Enter**.

> **TIP** Using IPCONFIG /registerdns refreshes a computer's A (host) record in DNS, which contains the IP address to name mapping for the host. IPCONFIG /registerdns does not reregister the SRV (service) records for a domain controller.

15. [handwritten note overlapping] ...ose the Command Prompt window.

16. [handwritten note overlapping] ...t intend to continue immediately to the next ...on.

Certificatio[n]

Objective: ... Planning, Implementing, and Maintaining a Microsoft ... rectory Infrastructure:

■ ...

REVIEW QUEST[IONS]

1. [blank] to manage the NetBIOS name cache.

2. [blank] to manage the DNS resolver cache.

3. You can use the _____ parameter of the NBTSTAT command to display the NetBIOS names of the local computer.

4. You can use the _____ parameter of the IPCONFIG command to display a computer's Host Name, Primary DNS Suffix, and other detailed information.

5. You can use the _____ file to map IP addresses to host names on the local computer.

[Handwritten note on index card:]
1. NBT stat
2. ipconfig /displaydns
3. -n
4. /All
5. LM hosts
   hosts

LAB 2.2 REFRESHING AND VERIFYING DOMAIN CONTROLLER DNS RECORDS

Objectives

The goal of this lab is to learn how the DNS records for a domain controller can be reregistered, and to verify that the DNS records for a domain controller have been registered correctly.

Materials Required

This lab will require the following:

- A Windows Server 2003 setup, as directed at the front of this lab manual

Estimated completion time: **10 minutes**

Activity Background

In order for Active Directory to function correctly, both clients and servers must be able to locate domain controllers on the network. When a Windows Server 2003 domain controller starts, it registers many records in DNS that allow it to be located by clients and other servers. In this lab you will learn how to manually refresh a domain controller's DNS records and then verify that the correct records have been registered. This can be useful when setting up a domain or reconfiguring your DNS infrastructure.

Activity

1. If necessary, start your server and log on using the **AdminXX** account in the **CHILDXX** domain (where *XX* is the number of your server) using the password **Password01**.

2. Click **Start**, select **Administrative Tools**, and then click **Services**.

3. In the right pane, scroll down and locate the Net Logon service as shown in Figure 2-3.

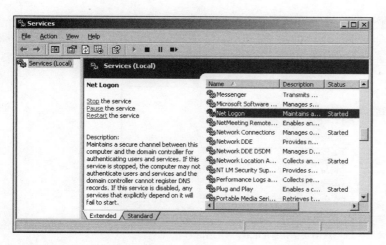

Figure 2-3   Net Logon service

4. Right-click **Net Logon** and then click **Restart**. This will stop the Net Logon service and then start it again.

 Restarting the Net Logon service may impact network users temporarily. In a production environment, the Net Logon service should only be restarted if you are experiencing network issues.

5. After the Net Logon service restarts, close the Services window.

6. Click **Start**, select **Administrative Tools**, and then click **DNS**.

7. In the left tree pane, expand the **Forward Lookup Zones** node and then double-click **child*XX*.supercorp.net** (where *XX* is the number of your server).

8. To confirm that the domain controller DNS records have been registered, locate the **_msdcs**, **_sites**, **_tcp**, and **_udp** subdomains as shown in Figure 2-4.

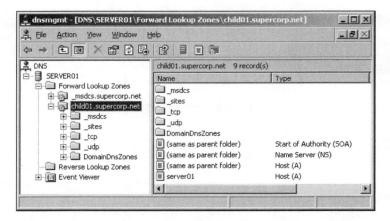

Figure 2-4   Forward Lookup Zones for the domain

9. Click **Start**, select **All Programs**, select **Accessories**, and then click **Notepad**.

10. In Notepad, click the **File** menu and then click **Open**.

11. In the File name drop-down list box, type **%SystemRoot%\system32\config\netlogon.dns** and then click **Open**. The netlogon.dns file contains the DNS resource records that the Net Logon service attempts to register in DNS. You can use the netlogon.dns file and the DNS management console to confirm that the correct records have been registered.

Note that you will need to select All Files from the Files of type drop-down list to actually see the netlogon.dns file in the Open dialog box.

NOTE

You can also use a tool called DNSLint to check domain controller DNS record registration. See Chapter 7 of this text, or Microsoft Knowledge Base articles 321045 and 321046 at support.microsoft.com, for more details on DNSLint.

TIP

12. Close Notepad and the DNS management console.

13. Log off your server if you do not intend to continue immediately to the next project. Otherwise, stay logged on.

Certification Objectives

Objectives for Microsoft Exam #70-294: Planning, Implementing, and Maintaining a Microsoft Windows Server 2003 Active Directory Infrastructure:

- Troubleshoot Active Directory.

REVIEW QUESTIONS

1. You can restart the _____ serv~~ice in order to reregister a domain~~ in controller's DNS records.

2. Which of the following subdomains wo~~uld be created if a~~ domain controller has registered records in DN~~S?~~

   a. _msdcs, _domains, _tcp, _ip

   b. _msdcs, _domains, _tcp, _udp

   c. _msdcs, _sites, _tcp, _ip

   d. _msdcs, _sites, _tcp, _udp

3. _____ contains a list of the reso~~urces that a controller~~ ller will attempt to register in DNS.

4. Running IPCONFIG /registerdns is e~~quivalent to restarting the Net L~~ogon service. True or False?

5. Restarting the Net Logon service may ~~take several minutes to complete~~ y. True or False?

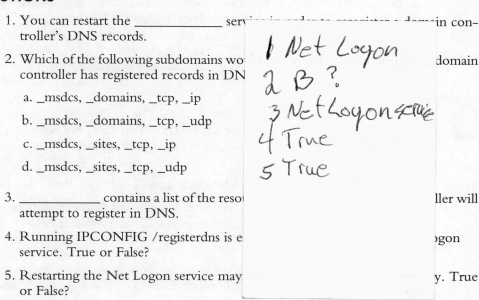

LAB 2.3 CREATING A PRIMARY AND SECONDARY FORWARD LOOKUP ZONE

Objectives

The goal of this lab is to learn how to create a primary and secondary forward lookup zone.

Materials Required

This lab will require the following:

- A Windows Server 2003 setup, as directed at the front of this lab manual

Estimated completion time: **15 minutes**

Activity Background

Second only to working with records within a zone, creating primary and secondary forward lookup zones is one of the main tasks a DNS administrator must know how to perform. Although a primary forward lookup zone to support Active Directory can be created automatically when the first domain controller is promoted, the administrator also has the option of creating the zone manually beforehand. Additionally, an administrator may decide to create secondary forward lookup zones on other DNS servers in order to improve query time. Finally, it may become necessary to add additional forward lookup zones that are used for tasks other than supporting Active Directory (such as a company intranet Web site). This lab will show you how to create both primary and secondary forward lookup zones.

ACTIVITY

Activity

1. If necessary, start your server and log on using the **AdminXX** account in the **CHILDXX** domain (where *XX* is the number of your server) using the password **Password01**.

2. Click **Start**, select **Administrative Tools**, and then click **DNS**.

3. In the left tree pane, right-click **Forward Lookup Zones** and click **New Zone**. The Welcome to the New Zone Wizard appears.

4. Click **Next**.

5. On the Zone Type screen, uncheck the **Store the zone in Active Directory** check box. This will store the zone in a file on the DNS server, rather than in Active Directory.

6. Leave the Primary zone option button selected and click **Next**.

7. On the Zone Name screen, enter **testdomainXX.local** (where *XX* is the number of your server) in the Zone name text box. Click **Next**.

8. On the Zone File screen, leave the default option that creates a new file named testdomain*XX*.local.dns for storing the DNS zone data. Click **Next**.

9. On the Dynamic Update screen, leave the default option, Do not allow dynamic updates, and click **Next**. The Completing the New Zone Wizard is displayed as shown in Figure 2-5.

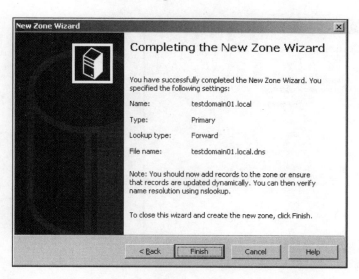

Figure 2-5   Completing the New Zone Wizard—Primary Zone

10. Click **Finish**. The new zone is displayed in the right details pane of the DNS management console. You have now created a primary forward lookup zone on your DNS server.

11. In the left tree pane, right-click **Forward Lookup Zones** and click **New Zone**. The Welcome to the New Zone Wizard appears.

12. Click **Next**.

13. On the Zone Type screen, select the **Secondary zone** option button and click **Next**.

14. On the Zone Name screen, enter **testdomainXX.local** (where *XX* is the number of your partner's server) in the Zone name text box. Click **Next**.

15. On the Master DNS Servers screen, enter **192.168.1.XX** (where *XX* is the last octet of your partner's server's IP address) and then click **Add**. Click **Next**. The Completing the New Zone Wizard is displayed as shown in Figure 2-6.

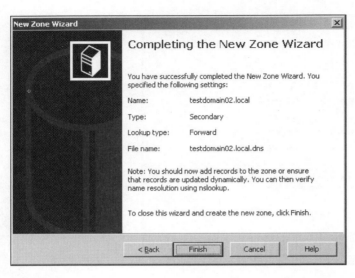

Figure 2-6　Completing the New Zone Wizard—Secondary Zone

16. Click **Finish**. The new zone is displayed in the right details pane of the DNS management console. You have now created a secondary forward lookup zone that is a replica of the primary zone on your partner's server.

Because Windows Server 2003 is configured to allow only zone transfers to DNS servers that have been added to the *name servers* list in the primary zone's properties, the zone transfer from the primary zone to the secondary zone will not occur until you have completed Lab 2.6. You may also receive an error that states that the zone could not be loaded by the DNS server. Complete Lab 2.6 to resolve this issue.

By default, Windows Server 2003 DNS servers hosting primary zones only allow servers on the *name servers* list to perform zone transfers from the primary zone. Servers hosting secondary zones do not allow zone transfers to other servers at all.

17. Close the DNS management console.

18. Log off your server if you do not intend to continue immediately to the next project. Otherwise, stay logged on.

Certification Objectives

Objectives for Microsoft Exam #70-294: Planning, Implementing, and Maintaining a Microsoft Windows Server 2003 Active Directory Infrastructure:

- Implement an Active Directory directory service forest and domain structure.

2

REVIEW QUESTIONS

1. Secondary zones can be stored in which of the following?

   a. Active Directory

   b. a file on the DNS server

   c. a file on the DNS server or in Active Directory

   d. a file not on the DNS server or in Active Directory

2. Secondary zones contain a writeable copy of a DNS zone. True or False?

3. By default, when hosting a primary zone, Windows Server 2003 DNS will allow zone transfers to which of the following?

   a. any DNS server that requests a zone transfer

   b. only DNS servers that are members of the same domain

   c. only DNS servers that are listed as name servers in the primary zone's properties

   d. no other DNS servers

4. By default, when hosting a secondary zone, Windows Server 2003 DNS will allow zone transfers to which of the following?

   a. any DNS server that requests a zone transfer

   b. only DNS servers that are members of the same domain

   c. only DNS servers that are listed as name servers in the primary zone's properties

   d. no other DNS servers

5. An authoritative DNS server is the same thing as a primary DNS server. True or False?

LAB 2.4 CREATING A PRIMARY REVERSE LOOKUP ZONE

Objectives

The goal of this lab is to learn how to create a primary reverse lookup zone.

Materials Required

This lab will require the following:

- A Windows Server 2003 setup, as directed at the front of this lab manual

Estimated completion time: **10 minutes**

Activity Background

Reverse lookup zones are used to resolve an IP address to a name—the opposite of a forward lookup zone. While most queries submitted to DNS are for resolving a name to an IP address, reverse lookups are used by many reporting and monitoring applications to provide information that is more user-friendly.

ACTIVITY

Activity

1. If necessary, start your server and log on using the **AdminXX** account in the **CHILDXX** domain (where *XX* is the number of your server) using the password **Password01**.

2. Click **Start**, select **Administrative Tools**, and then click **DNS**.

3. In the left tree pane, right-click **Reverse Lookup Zones** and click **New Zone**. The Welcome to the New Zone Wizard appears.

4. Click **Next**.

5. Leave the Primary zone option button selected and then uncheck the **Store the zone in Active Directory** check box. Click **Next**.

6. On the Reverse Lookup Zone Name screen, enter **192.168.1** in the Network ID text box as shown in Figure 2-7 and then click **Next**.

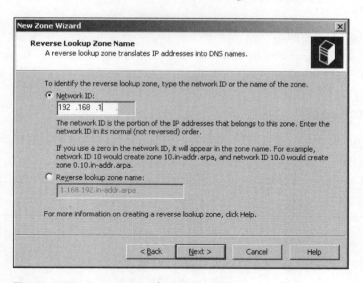

Figure 2-7   Reverse Lookup Zone Name

7. On the Zone File screen, leave the default option that creates a new file named 1.168.192.in-addr.arpa.dns for storing the DNS zone data. Click **Next**.

8. On the Dynamic Update screen, leave the default option (Do not allow dynamic updates) and click **Next**. The Completing the New Zone Wizard is displayed, as shown in Figure 2-8.

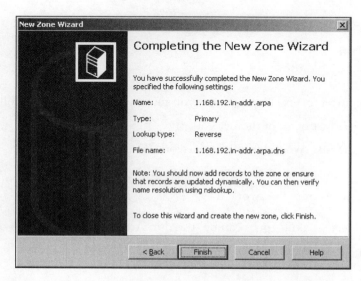

Figure 2-8   Completing the New Zone Wizard—Reverse Lookup Zone

9. Click **Finish**. The new zone is displayed in the right details pane of the DNS management console. You have now created a primary reverse lookup zone on your DNS server.

10. Close the DNS management console.

11. Log off your server if you do not intend to continue immediately to the next project. Otherwise, stay logged on.

Certification Objectives

Objectives for Microsoft Exam #70-294: Planning, Implementing, and Maintaining a Microsoft Windows Server 2003 Active Directory Infrastructure:

■ Implement an Active Directory directory service forest and domain structure.

REVIEW QUESTIONS

1. Reverse lookup zones are used for which of the following?

   a. to find the parent for a known FQDN

   b. to find the FQDN for a known parent

   c. to find the IP address for a known FQDN

   d. to find the FQDN for a known IP address

2. Which of the following domains was reserved for reverse lookups?

   a. in–arpa.addr

   b. arpa.in–addr

   c. in–addr.arpa

   d. in.addr.arpa

3. When creating a reverse lookup zone, you must specify which of the following?

   a. at least the first octet of the network ID

   b. at least the first two octets of the network ID

   c. at least the first three octets of the network ID

   d. all four octets of the network ID

4. Primary reverse lookup zones can be stored in Active Directory. True or False?

5. You can only create primary reverse lookup zones. True or False?

LAB 2.5 ADDING RECORDS TO A DNS ZONE

Objectives

The goal of this lab is to gain familiarity with the types of DNS resource records available.

Materials Required

This lab will require the following:

- A Windows Server 2003 setup, as directed at the front of this lab manual

Estimated completion time:**15 minutes**

Activity Background

In DNS, there are many different types of resource records that can be created by an administrator, each of which is used for a specific task. Host (A, also called "Address" or "Host Address") records are used to map a name to an IP address. Alias (CNAME) records are used to map a name to another name. Mail Exchanger (MX) records are used to specify the servers responsible for handling mail for the domain. Finally, Pointer (PTR) records are used to map an IP address to a name (that is, the reverse of a Host record). In this lab, you will learn how to create all four of these types of resource records using the DNS console.

Activity

1. If necessary, start your server and log on using the **AdminXX** account in the **CHILDXX** domain (where *XX* is the number of your server) using the password **Password01**.

2. Click **Start**, select **Administrative Tools**, and then click **DNS**.

3. In the left tree pane, expand the **Forward Lookup Zones** node and then click **testdomainXX.local** (where *XX* is the number of your server) to display the details for that zone in the right pane.

4. Right-click **testdomainXX.local** (where *XX* is the number of your server) in the left tree pane and click **New Host (A)**.

5. In the Name text box, enter **mail**. Note that the Fully qualified domain name text box updates to display the FQDN of the host.

6. In the IP address text box, enter **192.168.1.XX** (where *XX* is the last octet of your server's IP address), as shown in Figure 2-9.

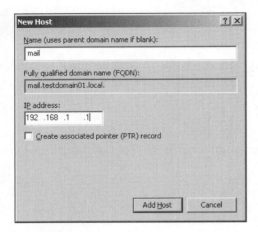

Figure 2-9   Creating a new Host (A) record

7. Click **Add Host**.

8. In the DNS message box, click **OK** to confirm the addition of the record.

9. Click **Done** on the New Hosts window to close the window. The new record for the mail host is now shown in the right details pane of the DNS management console.

10. Right-click **testdomainXX.local** (where *XX* is the number of your server) in the left tree pane and click **New Alias (CNAME)**.

11. In the Alias name text box, enter **smtp**.

12. In the Fully qualified domain name (FQDN) for target host text box, enter **mail.testdomainXX.local** (where *XX* is the number of your server). Alternatively, you can use the Browse button to locate the FQDN of the host.

13. Click **OK**. The new smtp alias record is now shown in the right details pane of the DNS management console.

14. Repeat Steps 10 to 13 using the alias **pop** and the FQDN **mail.testdomainXX.local** (where *XX* is the number of your server) to add an additional CNAME record.

15. Right-click **testdomainXX.local** (where *XX* is the number of your server) in the left tree pane and click **New Mail Exchanger (MX)**.

16. Leave the Host or child domain text box blank. By leaving this text box blank, the record will use the same name as the domain in which the record is contained.

17. In the Fully qualified domain name (FQDN) of mail server text box, enter **mail.testdomainXX.local** (where *XX* is the number of your server). Alternatively, you can use the Browse button to locate the FQDN of the host.

18. Click **OK**. The new mail exchanger record is now displayed in the right details pane of the DNS management console as shown in Figure 2-10.

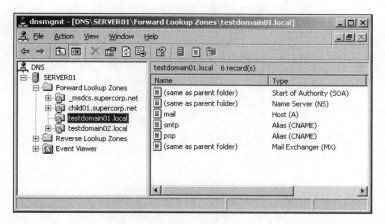

Figure 2-10   New records created in the testdomain*XX*.local zone

19. In the left tree pane, expand the **Reverse Lookup Zones** node and then click **192.168.1.x Subnet** to display the details for that zone in the right pane.

20. Right-click **192.168.1.x Subnet** and then click **New Pointer (PTR)**.

21. In the last octet of the Host IP number text box, enter the last octet of your server's IP address.

22. In the Host name text box, enter **mail.testdomainXX.local** (where *XX* is the number of your server) as shown in Figure 2-11. Alternatively, you can use the Browse button to locate the FQDN of the host.

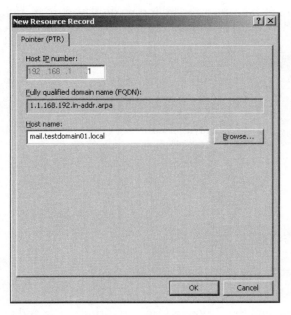

Figure 2-11   Creating a new Pointer (PTR) record

23. Click **OK**.

24. Close the DNS management console.

25. Log off your server if you do not intend to continue immediately to the next project. Otherwise, stay logged on.

Certification Objectives

Objectives for Microsoft Exam #70-294: Planning, Implementing, and Maintaining a Microsoft Windows Server 2003 Active Directory Infrastructure:

■ Implement an Active Directory directory service forest and domain structure.

■ Manage an Active Directory forest and domain structure.

REVIEW QUESTIONS

1. Use _____ records to map an FQDN to another FQDN.

2. Use _____ records to map an IP address to an FQDN.

3. Use _____ records to map an FQDN to an IP address.

2

4. MX records are used to specify which of the following?

   a. the servers that are responsible for handling mail for the domain

   b. the servers that are responsible for handling record exchanges for the domain

   c. the servers that are responsible for handling master exchanges for the domain

   d. the servers that are responsible for handling updates to the domain records

5. When creating a new Host (A) record, you do not have to specify a name for the host. True or False?

Lab 2.6 Modifying DNS Zone Settings

Objectives

The goal of this lab is to gain familiarity with some of the options available when configuring a DNS zone.

Materials Required

This lab will require the following:

- A Windows Server 2003 setup, as directed at the front of this lab manual

Estimated completion time: **10 minutes**

Activity Background

Once a zone is created, there are many options available. For example, a zone can be configured to store data in a file on the server or as objects in Active Directory. Additionally, a zone can be secured by only allowing computers that have been authorized on the network to add records to the zone. Settings are also available to control the removal of old records and to limit the amount of replication that occurs. In this lab you will learn how to configure these options.

Activity

1. If necessary, start your server and log on using the **AdminXX** account in the **CHILDXX** domain (where *XX* is the number of your server) using the password **Password01**.

2. Click **Start**, select **Administrative Tools**, and then click **DNS**.

3. In the left tree pane, expand the **Forward Lookup Zones** node and then click **testdomainXX.local** (where *XX* is the number of your server) to display the details for that zone in the right pane.

4. In the left tree pane, right-click **testdomainXX.local** (where *XX* is the number of your server) and then click **Properties**. Note the tabs available.

5. On the **General** tab, click **Change**.

6. To store the DNS zone data in Active Directory, rather than in a file on the DNS server, check the **Store the zone in Active Directory** check box on the Change Zone Type window as shown in Figure 2-12.

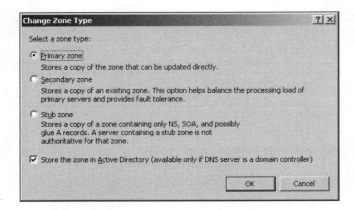

Figure 2-12   Change Zone Type window

7. Click **OK**.

8. When prompted if you want the zone to become Active Directory integrated, click **Yes**.

9. Click **Apply** on the testdomain*XX*.local Properties window to apply the change you have just made.

10. In the Dynamic updates drop-down list box, select **Secure only**. This will allow DNS records to be added to the zone by only authenticated users/computers.

11. Click **Aging**.

12. On the Zone Aging/Scavenging Properties window, check the **Scavenge stale resource records** checkbox to enable aging/scavenging as shown in Figure 2-13. Aging/scavenging helps to reduce the unnecessary replication of time stamp updates and the removal of old records.

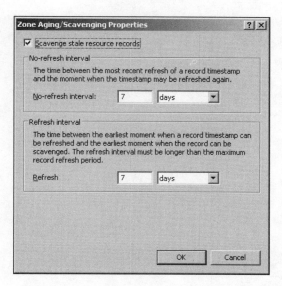

Figure 2-13   Zone Aging/Scavenging Properties window

NOTE

The No-refresh interval specifies the amount of time that must pass before a client can refresh the DNS record if the only property being updated is the time stamp. This prevents unnecessary replication from occurring when the client is only refreshing its DNS record(s). If the client updates another property of the record, such as the IP address the record should point to, the No-refresh interval is not applicable and the update is permitted. If a time stamp has not been updated, the Refresh interval specifies the amount of time after the No-refresh interval has expired, at which point a dynamically added record can be removed from the zone.

13. Click **OK**.

14. On the Name Servers tab, click **Add**.

15. In the Server fully qualified domain name text box, enter **SERVERXX.childXX.supercorp.net** (where *XX* is the number of your partner's server).

16. In the IP address text box, enter **192.168.1.XX** (where *XX* is the last octet of your partner's server's IP address) and click **Add**.

17. Click **OK**. The FQDN and IP address for your partner's server is added to the list of name servers that should be able to respond authoritatively for this zone, as shown in Figure 2-14.

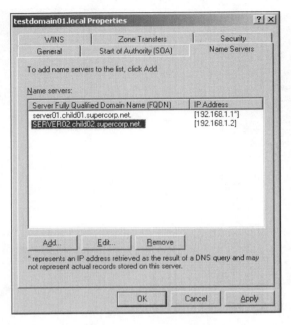

Figure 2-14   List of name servers for the zone

 Because the zone has been configured to allow only transfers to servers listed on the Name Servers tab by default, adding your partner's server to the name servers list is required. This will allow zone transfers to your partner's server, which is hosting a secondary copy of the zone. Alternatively, you can change the options on the Zone Transfers tab to allow zone transfers for this zone to any server that requests a transfer.

18. Click **OK** on the testdomain*XX*.local Properties window to save the changes you have just made and close the window.

19. Close the DNS management console.

20. Log off your server.

Certification Objectives

Objectives for Microsoft Exam #70-294: Planning, Implementing, and Maintaining a Microsoft Windows Server 2003 Active Directory Infrastructure:

■ Manage an Active Directory forest and domain structure.

REVIEW QUESTIONS

1. Zones that store their data in Active Directory, rather than in a file on the DNS server, are called which of the following?

   a. Active Directory-stored

   b. Active Directory-integrated

   c. Active Directory-standard

   d. Active Directory-DNS

2. When dynamic updates are set to _____, a user/computer must be authenticated in order to add records to the DNS zone.

3. After adding a secondary zone and attempting to view its details, you receive an error message stating that the zone could not be loaded by the DNS server. Which of the following is one way to correct the issue?

   a. Add the secondary server's FQDN and IP address on the Name Servers tab in the primary server's zone properties.

   b. Add the primary server's FQDN and IP address on the Name Servers tab in the secondary server's zone properties.

   c. Add the secondary server's FQDN and IP address on the Zone Transfers tab in the primary server's zone properties.

   d. Add the primary server's FQDN and IP address on the Zone Transfers tab in the secondary server's zone properties.

4. The _____ interval specifies the amount of time after the No-refresh interval expires that a dynamically registered record can be removed from a DNS zone if it is not refreshed.

5. You can use the _____ interval to control the amount of time that must pass before a dynamically registered record can be refreshed in DNS.

ACTIVE DIRECTORY DESIGN PHILOSOPHY

Labs included in this chapter:

♦ Lab 3.1 Locating Additional MSF Information

♦ Lab 3.2 Locating Additional MOF Information

♦ Lab 3.3 Locating the Windows Server 2003 Deployment Kit

♦ Lab 3.4 Identifying and Setting the Manager of a Directory Object

♦ Lab 3.5 Querying Active Directory about Managers

Microsoft MCSE Exam #70-294 Objectives	
Objective	Lab
Implement an Active Directory directory service forest and domain structure.	3.1, 3.3, 3.4, 3.5
Implement an Active Directory site topology.	3.1, 3.3
Plan an administrative delegation strategy.	3.1, 3.3, 3.4, 3.5
Manage an Active Directory forest and domain structure.	3.2, 3.4, 3.5
Manage an Active Directory site.	3.2
Plan an OU structure.	3.1, 3.3, 3.4, 3.5

Lab 3.1 Locating Additional MSF Information

Objectives

The goal of this lab is to learn where additional information on the Microsoft Solutions Framework (MSF) can be found.

Materials Required

This lab will require the following:

- A Windows Server 2003 setup, as directed at the front of this lab manual

- A connection to the Internet

Estimated completion time: **10 minutes**

Activity Background

A project managed according to the philosophy of MSF goes through a number of stages leading to a product's release. The common MSF stages are envisioning, planning, developing, stabilizing, and deploying. Although MSF is ideally suited to the business of creating and publishing software, MSF can easily be applied to an Active Directory project. In this lab you will download and review a document from Microsoft's Web site that covers the MSF process model.

ACTIVITY

Activity

1. If necessary, start your server and log on using the **AdminXX** account in the **CHILDXX** domain (where *XX* is the number of your server) using the password **Password01**.

2. Click **Start**, select **All Programs**, and then click **Internet Explorer**.

3. On the Tools menu, click **Internet Options**.

4. Click the **Security** tab.

5. With **Internet** selected, move the slider down to **Medium** in the Security level for this zone.

If a slider does not appear, you may need to click the "Default Level" button. You can then move the slider from High to Medium.

TIP

6. Click **Yes** when the Warning! message box appears.

7. Click **OK** to close Internet Options.

By default, the security level for Internet Explorer in Windows Server 2003 is set to high. While in a production environment it is recommended you leave this default value, it can interfere with the advanced functionality of many Web sites.

8. In the Address bar, enter *www.microsoft.com/msf* and then click **Go**.

9. In the right pane, click the **MSF Resource Library** link.

10. Locate and click the link to the document entitled **MSF Process Model**. If desired, read the document. You will use information from this document to answer the review questions.

It is not uncommon for the Microsoft Web site to be reorganized. If you are unable to locate the document by following these steps, use the search feature on Microsoft's Web site to search for the document.

11. Close Internet Explorer and log off your server if you do not intend to continue immediately to the next project. Otherwise, stay logged on.

Certification Objectives

Objectives for Microsoft Exam #70-294: Planning, Implementing, and Maintaining a Microsoft Windows Server 2003 Active Directory Infrastructure:

- Implement an Active Directory directory service forest and domain structure.

- Implement an Active Directory site topology.

- Plan an administrative delegation strategy.

- Plan an OU structure.

REVIEW QUESTIONS

1. The _____ model focuses on the continual need to refine the requirements and estimates for a project.

2. The _____ model uses milestones as transition and assessment points.

3. A _____ is a measurement or known state by which something is measured or compared.

4. The "Tradeoff Triangle" refers to the relationship between the project variables of resources, schedule, and _____.

5. During the _____ interim milestone, the team will test as much of the entire solution in as true a production environment as possible.

LAB 3.2 LOCATING ADDITIONAL MOF INFORMATION

Objectives

The goal of this lab is to learn where additional information on the Microsoft Operations Framework (MOF) can be found.

Materials Required

This lab will require the following:

- A Windows Server 2003 setup, as directed at the front of this lab manual

- A connection to the Internet

Estimated completion time: **10 minutes**

Activity Background

While MSF deals with the creation of new software and new systems, MOF deals with the effective management of existing systems, particularly core Microsoft enterprise offerings. MOF consists of a series of guidelines, best practices, and how-to guides that maximize the availability and performance of a network and its components. In this lab you will download and review a document from Microsoft's Web site that covers the MOF process model.

ACTIVITY

Activity

1. If necessary, start your server and log on using the **AdminXX** account in the **CHILDXX** domain (where *XX* is the number of your server) using the password **Password01**.

2. Click **Start**, select **All Programs**, and then click **Internet Explorer**.

3. In the Address bar, enter *www.microsoft.com/mof* and then click **Go**.

4. In the right pane, click the **MOF Resource Library** link.

5. Locate the link to the document entitled **MOF Process Model for Operations** (the link may be called *MOF Process Model*). If desired, read the document. You will use information from this document to answer the review questions.

> It is not uncommon for the Microsoft Web site to be reorganized. If you are unable to locate the document by following these steps, use the search feature on Microsoft's Web site to search for the document.

6. Close Internet Explorer and log off your server if you do not intend to continue immediately to the next project. Otherwise, stay logged on.

Certification Objectives

Objectives for Microsoft Exam #70-294: Planning, Implementing, and Maintaining a Microsoft Windows Server 2003 Active Directory Infrastructure:

- Manage an Active Directory forest and domain structure.

- Manage an Active Directory site.

REVIEW QUESTIONS

1. In the _____ quadrant, new service solutions, technologies, systems, applications, hardware, and processes are introduced.

2. The _____ quadrant is concerned with executing day-to-day tasks effectively and efficiently.

3. The _____ quadrant is concerned with resolving incidents, problems, and inquiries quickly.

4. The _____ quadrant drives changes to optimize cost, performance, capacity, and availability in the delivery of IT services.

5. A _____ is any change, or group of changes, that must be incorporated into a managed IT environment.

LAB 3.3 LOCATING THE WINDOWS SERVER 2003 DEPLOYMENT KIT

Objectives

The goal of this lab is to learn where the Windows Server 2003 Deployment Kit can be found.

Materials Required

This lab will require the following:

- A Windows Server 2003 setup, as directed at the front of this lab manual

- A connection to the Internet

> Estimated completion time: **10 minutes**

Activity Background

Although a team can use MSF directly to deploy Active Directory, Microsoft has also created a deployment kit for Windows Server 2003 based on MSF. The Windows Server 2003 Deployment Kit contains many detailed planning guides to ensure a smooth deployment of Windows Server 2003, including Active Directory. In this lab you will access the Windows Server 2003 Deployment Kit and review the chapter covering Active Directory deployment.

Activity

1. If necessary, start your server and log on using the **AdminXX** account in the **CHILDXX** domain (where *XX* is the number of your server) using the password **Password01**.

2. Click **Start**, select **All Programs**, and then click **Internet Explorer**.

3. In the Address bar, enter *www.microsoft.com/windows2003* and then click **Go**.

4. In the left menu, click **Technical Resources**. (Note: you may need to select Technical Resources: Overview if a menu displays when you click Technical Resources.)

5. Under the Product Documentation heading, click the **Windows Server 2003 Deployment Guide** link.

It is not uncommon for the Microsoft Web site to be reorganized. If you are unable to locate the deployment kit by following these steps, use the search feature on Microsoft's Web site to search for the kit.

6. Under the Designing and Deploying Directory and Security Services section, click the **Download this book** link.

7. Under the Files in this Download heading, click the **04_CHAPTER_1_ Planning_an_Active_Directory_Deployment_Project.doc** link.

8. When prompted if you would like to save or open the file, click **Open**. The document will then open in WordPad or another word processing application, depending on the software installed on your server. If desired, read the document. You will use information from this document to answer the review questions.

9. After answering the review questions, close the document (do not save any changes), close Internet Explorer, and log off your server if you do not intend to continue immediately to the next project. Otherwise, stay logged on.

Certification Objectives

Objectives for Microsoft Exam #70-294: Planning, Implementing, and Maintaining a Microsoft Windows Server 2003 Active Directory Infrastructure:

- Implement an Active Directory directory service forest and domain structure.

- Implement an Active Directory site topology.

- Plan an administrative delegation strategy.

- Plan an OU structure.

REVIEW QUESTIONS

1. During the _____ phase, the design team creates a design for the Active Directory logical structure that best meets the needs of each division in the organization that will use the directory service.

2. The process of upgrading the directory service of a domain to a later version of the directory service is called a _____.

3. The _____ topology is a logical representation of your physical network.

4. The _____ of your existing environment determines your strategy for deploying Windows Server 2003 Active Directory.

5. _____ testing is the first evaluation of the Active Directory design.

LAB 3.4 IDENTIFYING AND SETTING THE MANAGER OF A DIRECTORY OBJECT

Objectives

The goal of this lab is to learn how Active Directory can be used to identify the managers of objects in the directory.

Materials Required

This lab will require the following:

- A Windows Server 2003 setup, as directed at the front of this lab manual

Estimated completion time: **10 minutes**

Activity Background

Data owners, also called object owners, are responsible for the contents of the directory. They create, modify, delete, and manage objects in the directory, such as organizational units. Using Active Directory Users and Computers, a manager (that is, data owner) can be assigned to many objects in the directory. Specifying a manager allows users and administrators to clearly identify which person or organization is responsible for a given portion of the directory. This lab walks you through the steps needed to view and set the manager of an object.

Activity

1. If necessary, start your server and log on using the **AdminXX** account in the **CHILDXX** domain (where *XX* is the number of your server) using the password **Password01**.

2. Click **Start**, select **Administrative Tools**, and then click **Active Directory Users and Computers**.

3. If necessary, in the left tree pane, expand the **childXX.supercorp.net** (where *XX* is the number of your server) node.

4. In the left tree pane, click the **Domain Controllers** OU.

5. In the right details pane, right-click **SERVERXX** (where *XX* is the number of your server) and then click **Properties**.

6. Click the **Managed By** tab.

NOTE

In a project where an existing Active Directory infrastructure is already in place, you can use the Managed By tab to identify the manager of an object if one has been set. Because this directory has been recently created, the information on the Managed By tab will most likely not be set.

7. Click the **Change** button.

8. On the Select User or Contact window, enter **AdminXX** (where *XX* is the number of your server) in the Enter the object name to select text box, as shown in Figure 3-1.

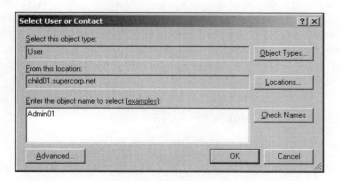

Figure 3-1   Select User or Contact window

9. Click **OK**.

10. The SERVER*XX* Properties Managed By tab updates to show Admin*XX* as the new owner/manager of the object, as shown in Figure 3-2. Note that other fields on the tab are still blank. This is because the Admin*XX* account properties have not been set with any of this information.

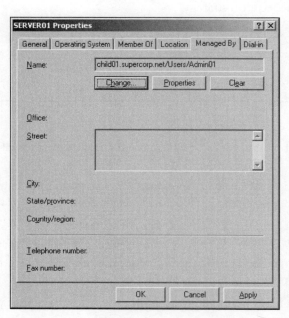

Figure 3-2   SERVER*XX* Properties Managed By tab

Do not get confused with setting a user account as the manager of an object and giving a user account permissions to manage an object. The information on the Managed By tab is only used for identifying the logical manager (or owner) of the object. It does not give users any security access to the object (except in the case of managers of *groups,* who can be given permissions to modify group memberships directly on the Managed By tab). For a user to access or modify an object, security permissions on the object must be set specifically using the object's Access Control List. The labs in Chapter 9 cover object permissions in more detail.

11. Click **OK** to close the SERVER*XX* Properties window.

12. Close the Active Directory Users and Computers console.

13. Log off your server if you do not intend to continue immediately to the next project. Otherwise, stay logged on.

Certification Objectives

Objectives for Microsoft Exam #70-294: Planning, Implementing, and Maintaining a Microsoft Windows Server 2003 Active Directory Infrastructure:

- Implement an Active Directory directory service forest and domain structure.

- Plan an administrative delegation strategy.

- Manage an Active Directory forest and domain structure.

- Plan an OU structure.

REVIEW QUESTIONS

1. The _____ tab in an object's properties contains information about the manager of an object.

2. After setting the manager of an object in Active Directory, you notice that only the Name field contains information. What is the most likely reason for the other fields to be blank?

   a. You do not have permission to view the details of the manager's user account.

   b. You must reopen the object's Properties before the other fields on the Managed By tab will update.

   c. The fields are most likely blank in the account properties of the user you have set as the manager.

   d. The fields do not automatically update, and must be entered manually.

3. The "Managed By" attribute of an object and having permissions to manage an object are equivalent. True or False?

4. An object such as a computer account or organizational unit can have only one user account set on the Managed By tab. True or False?

5. All objects in the directory must have the "Managed By" attribute set before they can be created. True or False?

3

LAB 3.5 QUERYING ACTIVE DIRECTORY ABOUT MANAGERS

Objectives

The goal of this lab is to learn how to create a saved query that will return all the objects that are managed by a given user account in Active Directory.

Materials Required

This lab will require the following:

- A Windows Server 2003 setup, as directed at the front of this lab manual

Estimated completion time:**10 minutes**

Activity Background

In Chapter 1 you learned how to create a saved query that returned all user accounts with passwords that never expire. In this lab, you will learn more about the versatility of saved queries by creating a custom query that returns all objects managed by a given user account.

ACTIVITY

Activity

1. If necessary, start your server and log on using the **AdminXX** account in the **CHILDXX** domain (where *XX* is the number of your server) using the password **Password01**.

2. Click **Start**, select **Administrative Tools**, and then click **Active Directory Users and Computers**.

3. In the left tree pane, right-click **Saved Queries**, select **New**, and then click **Query**.

4. In the Name text box, enter **Objects Managed by AdminXX** (where *XX* is the number of your server).

5. Click the **Define Query** button.

6. In the Find drop-down list box, select **Custom Search**.

7. Click the **Advanced** tab.

8. In the Enter LDAP query text box, type **(managedBy=CN=AdminXX,CN=Users,DC=childXX, DC=supercorp,DC=net)** (where *XX* is the number of your server) as shown in Figure 3-3.

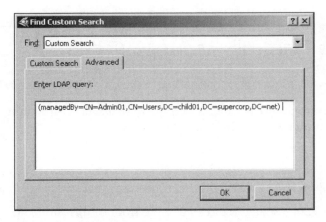

Figure 3-3   Find Custom Search window

9. Click **OK**.

10. On the New Query window, click **OK**. The query you have just created appears as shown in Figure 3-4. If the results are not automatically displayed on your server, expand the Saved Queries folder in the left tree pane and then click Objects Managed by Admin*XX* (where *XX* is the number of your server).

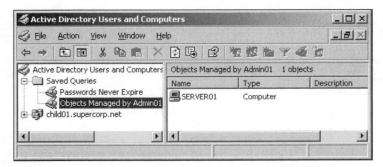

Figure 3-4   Objects Managed by Admin*XX* query

11. Close the Active Directory Users and Computers console.

12. Log off your server.

Certification Objectives

Objectives for Microsoft Exam #70-294: Planning, Implementing, and Maintaining a Microsoft Windows Server 2003 Active Directory Infrastructure:

3

- Implement an Active Directory directory service forest and domain structure.

- Plan an administrative delegation strategy.

- Manage an Active Directory forest and domain structure.

- Plan an OU structure.

REVIEW QUESTIONS

1. The _____ attribute of a directory object identifies who is logically responsible for the object.

2. Which of the following LDAP queries would you use to find all objects that were managed by a user account named Pat, located in the Marketing organizational unit of the mydomain.com domain?

   a. (managedBy=DC=com,DC=mydomain,CN=Marketing,CN=Pat)

   b. (managedBy=CN=Pat,CN=Marketing,DC=mydomain,DC=com)

   c. (managedBy=DC=com,DC=mydomain,OU=Marketing,CN=Pat)

   d. (managedBy=CN=Pat,OU=Marketing,DC=mydomain,DC=com)

3. The LDAP query (managedBy=*) will return:

   a. all objects that have a manager set

   b. all objects that do not have a manager set

   c. all objects that do or do not have a manager set

   d. all objects that are managed by a user account called *

4. When referring to an Organizational Unit in a distinguished name, the two-character identifier _____ is used.

5. When referring to a Container in a distinguished name, the two-character identifier _____ is used.

4

ACTIVE DIRECTORY ARCHITECTURE

Labs included in this chapter:

- ◆ Lab 4.1 Creating an Auxiliary Class
- ◆ Lab 4.2 Adding an Auxiliary Class to a Structural Class
- ◆ Lab 4.3 Modifying an Attribute
- ◆ Lab 4.4 Schema Modification Using LDIFDE
- ◆ Lab 4.5 Reloading the Schema Cache and Viewing Permissions
- ◆ Lab 4.6 Locating the Guide to Securing the Schema

Microsoft MCSE Exam #70-294 Objectives	
Objective	Lab
Implement an Active Directory directory service forest and domain structure.	4.1, 4.2, 4.4
Manage an Active Directory forest and domain structure.	4.3, 4.4, 4.5
Troubleshoot Active Directory.	4.4, 4.5

Lab 4.1 Creating an Auxiliary Class

Objectives

The goal of this lab is to learn how to create an Auxiliary Class in the Active Directory Schema.

Materials Required

This lab will require the following:

- A Windows Server 2003 setup, as directed at the front of this lab manual

- A Microsoft Management Console with the Schema snap-in added and saved to the desktop

Estimated completion time:**10 minutes**

Activity Background

Auxiliary classes contain a list of attributes that you can add to the class definition of a Structural class, Abstract class, or that can be inherited by another Auxiliary class. Auxiliary classes are most useful when you have a set of attributes that need to be added to several classes, but you can't use inheritance. You will create a new Auxiliary class in this lab for use in Lab 4.2.

Activity

1. If necessary, start your server and log on using the **Administrator** account in the **SUPERCORP** domain using the password **Password01**.

Because modifying the schema has consequences across all domains in the entire forest, only members of Schema Admins have permission to modify the schema by default. Schema Admins is a group located in the forest root domain. The default Administrator account in the forest root domain is automatically a member of Schema Admins.

2. On the desktop, double-click the **Schema console** you have already created that contains the Active Directory Schema snap-in.

3. In the left tree pane, expand the **Active Directory Schema** node.

4. Create two new attributes using the details shown below. For the Common Name and LDAP Display Name, substitute *XX* with the number of your server. Also, substitute *XX* in the Unique X500 Object ID with the number of your server, but without any leading zeros.

Attribute One

Common Name: **Supercorp-Com-2004-MAN-SSN-*XX***

LDAP Display Name: **Supercorp-Com-2004-manSSN*XX***

Unique X500 Object ID:
1.2.840.113556.1.5.7000.111.28688.28684.8.87165.*XX*.2

Description: **Social Security Number**

Syntax: **Numerical String**

Minimum: **9**

Maximum: **9**

Attribute Two

Common Name: **Supercorp-Com-2004-MAN-Salary-*XX***

LDAP Display Name: **Supercorp-Com-2004-manSalary*XX***

Unique X500 Object ID:
1.2.840.113556.1.5.7000.111.28688.28684.8.87165.*XX*.3

Description: **Staff member salary**

Syntax: **Integer**

NOTE

If you receive the error "The FSMO role ownership could not be verified because its directory partition has not replicated successfully with at least one replication partner" when attempting to create the attributes, you have most likely just turned on your server. In order for a domain controller to determine the current schema master after being shut down, it must perform replication with one of its partners. Wait 5 to 15 minutes for replication to occur and then try creating the attributes again. Alternatively, your instructor may provide you with steps for manually initiating replication (this is covered in Chapter 6).

5. In the left tree pane, right-click **Classes** and then click **Create Class**. A message box informs you that schema objects cannot be deleted once they are created. They can only be disabled.

6. Click **Continue**. The Create New Schema Class window displays.

7. In the Common Name text box, enter **Supercorp-Com-2004-MAN-Staff-Info-XX** (where *XX* is the number of your server).

8. In the LDAP Display Name text box, enter **Supercorp-Com-2004-manStaffInfoXX** (where *XX* is the number of your server).

9. In the Unique X500 Object ID text box, enter **1.2.840.113556.1.5.7000.111.28688.28684.8.87986.XX.2** (where *XX* is the number of your server, without any leading zeros).

10. In the Description text box, enter **Information for all staff classes**.

11. In the Class Type drop-down list box, select **Auxiliary**. Your screen should look similar to Figure 4-1.

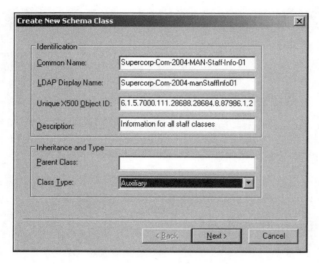

Figure 4-1 Creating a new Auxiliary Class

 NOTE If you do not specify a parent class when creating a new class, the new class will automatically have the Abstract Class called *top* set as its parent class. All objects in Active Directory inherit from the class *top* (directly or indirectly).

12. Click **Next**.

13. Next to the Optional attributes list box, click **Add**.

14. Select **Supercorp-Com-2004-manSalaryXX** (where *XX* is the number of your server) and click **OK**.

15. Next to the Optional attributes list box, click **Add**.

16. Select **Supercorp-Com-2004-manSSNXX** (where *XX* is the number of your server) and click **OK**. Your screen should appear similar to Figure 4-2.

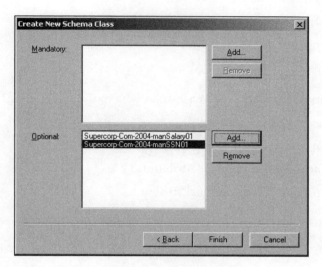

Figure 4-2   Adding attributes to an Auxiliary Class

17. Click **Finish**. Your new Auxiliary Class has been created.

18. Close the Microsoft Management Console that contains the Active Directory Schema snap-in. If prompted to save changes, click **No**.

19. Log off your server if you do not intend to continue immediately to the next project. Otherwise, stay logged on.

Certification Objectives

Objectives for Microsoft Exam #70-294: Planning, Implementing, and Maintaining a Microsoft Windows Server 2003 Active Directory Infrastructure:

■ Implement an Active Directory directory service forest and domain structure.

REVIEW QUESTIONS

1. Which of the following is not true?

   a. Auxiliary classes can be derived from other Auxiliary classes.

   b. Abstract classes can be derived from other Abstract classes.

   c. Structural classes can be derived from Abstract classes.

   d. Structural classes can be derived from Auxiliary classes.

2. All objects in Active Directory inherit from the _____ class.

3. An Auxiliary Class can be derived from which of the following?

   a. An Auxiliary class

   b. An Abstract class

   c. An Auxiliary class or an Abstract class

   d. Neither an Auxiliary class nor an Abstract class

4. Once an Auxiliary Class is created, you can do which of the following?

   a. Add additional mandatory attributes.

   b. Add additional optional attributes.

   c. Add both mandatory and optional attributes.

   d. Add neither mandatory nor optional attributes.

5. Two schema objects in Active Directory can have the same X500 object ID. True or False?

LAB 4.2 ADDING AN AUXILIARY CLASS TO A STRUCTURAL CLASS

Objectives

The goal of this lab is to learn how to add an Auxiliary Class to the class definition of a Structural Class.

Materials Required

This lab will require the following:

- A Windows Server 2003 setup, as directed at the front of this lab manual

- A Microsoft Management Console with the Schema snap-in added and saved to the desktop

Estimated completion time: **10 minutes**

Activity Background

Once a class is defined, you can no longer add mandatory attributes to the class (unless you deactivate and redefine the class). However, you can add or remove optional attributes to and from the class definition as needed. In this lab, you will add the Auxiliary class created in Lab 4.1 (which contains only optional attributes) to a Structural class created in the main text associated with this lab manual.

Activity

1. If necessary, start your server and log on using the **Administrator** account in the **SUPERCORP** domain using the password **Password01**.

2. On the desktop, double-click the **Schema console** you have already created that contains the Active Directory Schema snap-in.

3. In the left tree pane, expand the **Active Directory Schema** node.

4. In the left tree pane, expand the **Classes** node.

5. In the left tree pane, right-click **Supercorp-Com-2004-manStaffXX** (where *XX* is the number of your server) and then click **Properties**.

6. Click the **Relationship** tab.

7. Click **Add Class**.

8. Select **Supercorp-Com-2004-manStaffInfoXX** (where *XX* is the number of your server) and click **OK**. Your screen should look similar to Figure 4-3.

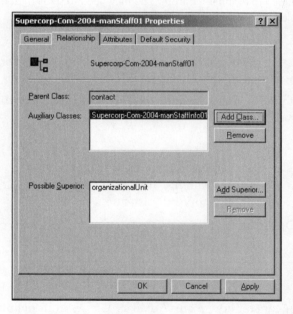

Figure 4-3   Adding an Auxiliary Class to the definition of a Structural Class

9. Click **OK** to close the Supercorp-Com-2004-manStaffXX Properties window.

10. With **Supercorp-Com-2004-manStaffXX** (where *XX* is the number of your server) selected in the left tree pane, notice that the attributes from the Supercorp-Com-2004-manStaffInfo*XX* Auxiliary Class now appear in the right details pane, as shown in Figure 4-4.

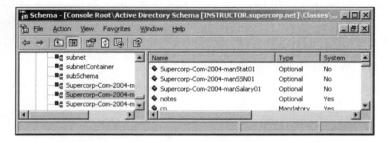

Figure 4-4   Additional attributes in the Supercorp-Com-2004-manStaff*XX* class

Use the Source Class column in the right details pane to identify which class an attribute was added to or inherited from. You may need to scroll right or maximize the console in order to view this column.

11. Close the Microsoft Management Console that contains the Active Directory Schema snap-in. If prompted to save changes, click **No**.

12. Log off your server if you do not intend to continue immediately to the next project. Otherwise, stay logged on.

Certification Objectives

Objectives for Microsoft Exam #70-294: Planning, Implementing, and Maintaining a Microsoft Windows Server 2003 Active Directory Infrastructure:

■ Implement an Active Directory directory service forest and domain structure.

REVIEW QUESTIONS

1. A Structural Class can contain how many Auxiliary Classes in its definition?

a. None

b. One

c. Multiple

d. Number is dependent on whether the Auxiliary class was derived from another Auxiliary class

2. A Structural Class can be derived from how many Auxiliary Classes?

   a. None

   b. One

   c. Multiple

   d. Number is dependent on whether the Auxiliary class was derived from another Auxiliary class

3. You can use the _____ column in the Active Directory Schema snap-in to identify where an attribute was added to a class.

4. You can add multiple Abstract Classes to the definition of a Structural Class in the same way you can add multiple Auxiliary Classes. True or False?

5. _____ Classes, Structural Classes, and 88 Classes are the only class types from which a Structural Class can inherit.

4

LAB 4.3 MODIFYING AN ATTRIBUTE

Objectives

The goal of this lab is to learn how to modify an attribute so it is indexed and stored in the Global Catalog.

Materials Required

This lab will require the following:

- A Windows Server 2003 setup, as directed at the front of this lab manual

- A Microsoft Management Console with the Schema snap-in added and saved to the desktop

Estimated completion time: **5 minutes**

Activity Background

Overall, the default objects in the Active Directory Schema are configured for the best performance in the majority of situations. However, you may have custom attributes or possibly even one or more default attributes that can benefit from being indexed or stored in the Global Catalog. Using one of the attributes you created in Lab 4.1, in this lab you will learn how to enable indexing for an attribute and how to store attributes in the Global Catalog.

Activity

1. If necessary, start your server and log on using the **Administrator** account in the **SUPERCORP** domain using the password **Password01**.

2. On the desktop, double-click the **Schema console** you have already created that contains the Active Directory Schema snap-in.

3. In the left tree pane, expand the **Active Directory Schema** node.

4. In the left tree pane, click **Attributes** to display a list of all attributes in the right details pane.

5. In the right details pane, right-click **Supercorp-Com-2004-manSSNXX** and then click **Properties**.

6. Check the box next to **Index this attribute in the Active Directory**.

TIP

You can use the *Index this attribute for containerized searches in the Active Directory* check box to create an index on this attribute for each container in Active Directory. This can speed up searches that specify a specific container, because typically only a smaller container index needs to be used, rather than a larger index of the entire Active Directory. However, keep in mind that additional resources are required to store and maintain the index.

7. Check the box next to **Replicate this attribute to the Global Catalog**. Your screen should look similar to Figure 4-5.

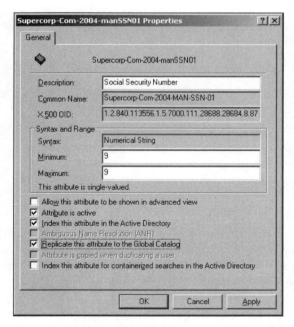

Figure 4-5   Modifying settings on an attribute

8. Click **OK**.

9. Close the Microsoft Management Console that contains the Active Directory Schema snap-in. If prompted to save changes, click **No**.

10. Log off your server if you do not intend to continue immediately to the next project. Otherwise, stay logged on.

Certification Objectives

Objectives for Microsoft Exam #70-294: Planning, Implementing, and Maintaining a Microsoft Windows Server 2003 Active Directory Infrastructure:

■ Manage an Active Directory forest and domain structure.

REVIEW QUESTIONS

1. You can _____ an attribute in order to improve query performance on that attribute.

2. The _____ contains every object in the forest, but with a limited subset of the objects' attributes.

3. When selecting an attribute to index, you should look for which of the following?

   a. low selectivity

   b. mid selectivity

   c. high selectivity

   d. Selectivity does not matter.

4. You should index every possible attribute you will ever search on. True or False?

5. Storing attributes in the global catalog will have what effect on cross-domain network traffic?

   a. It will raise replication traffic, but lower query traffic.

   b. It will lower replication traffic and query traffic.

   c. It will lower replication traffic, but increase query traffic.

   d. It will have no effect on replication traffic or query traffic.

LAB 4.4 SCHEMA MODIFICATION USING LDIFDE

Objectives

The goal of this lab is to learn how you can use the LDIFDE utility to modify the Active Directory Schema by using an LDAP Interchange Format (LDIF) file.

Materials Required

This lab will require the following:

- A Windows Server 2003 setup, as directed at the front of this lab manual

- A Microsoft Management Console with the Schema snap-in added and saved to the desktop

- Optionally, a connection to the Internet

Estimated completion time: **10 minutes**

Activity Background

While the Active Directory Schema snap-in allows an administrator to manually edit the schema, LDIFDE is another utility that can also be used to create or modify classes and attributes in the schema. One benefit of using LDIFDE is that the administrator applying the changes to the schema does not need to know how to use the Active Directory Schema snap-in (or be informed about how the schema works, for that matter). Additionally, using an LDIF file can ensure that the exact same changes are made in two or more different Active Directory installations (such as when you have a test/dev environment and a production environment). In this lab, you will create an LDIF file that removes the Auxiliary class created in Lab 4.1 from the Structural class it was added to in Lab 4.2. Note that, although this lab focuses on using LDIFDE to modify the schema, you can use LDIFDE to modify other objects in Active Directory as well.

Activity

1. If necessary, start your server and log on using the **Administrator** account in the **SUPERCORP** domain using the password **Password01**.

2. Click **Start**, select **All Programs**, select **Accessories**, and then click **Notepad**.

Keep in mind that the classes and attributes that make up the schema are also objects in Active Directory. Each class or attribute you create is an object stored in the schema naming context. Connecting to the schema naming context by using ADSI Edit, you can view the schema objects and their attributes.

3. Type the following text into notepad (substituting *XX* with the number of your server), as shown in Figure 4-6:

dn:.CN=Supercorp–Com–2004–MAN–Staff–*XX*,CN=Schema,CN= Configuration, DC=supercorp,DC=net

changetype: modify

delete: auxiliaryClass

auxiliaryClass: Supercorp–Com–2004–manStaffInfo*XX*

-

The Distinguished Name (DN) should all be on one line. Additionally, do not forget the trailing hyphen (-).

CAUTION

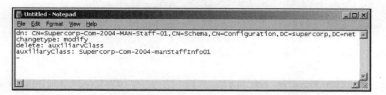

Figure 4-6   Example LDIFDE file to remove Auxiliary Class

The first line of this file specifies the Distinguished Name (DN) of the object to be added or modified. In this case, we want to modify the *Supercorp-Com-2004-MAN-Staff-XX* object, which is located in the schema naming context. The next line of the file, *changetype*, specifies the type of operation to be performed on the object. Other valid values for *changetype* include *add*, to create a new object with the specified DN; and *delete*, to delete an object with the specified DN.

NOTE

When you specify *modify* as the *changetype*, you can specify one or more operations to be performed on the object's attributes. Valid operations include *add*, to add a new value to an attribute; *replace*, to replace an existing value; and *delete*, to remove an existing value. You must separate each operation by a hyphen (-). In this example, we are deleting the *Supercorp-Com-2004-manStaffInfoXX* value from the *auxiliaryClass* attribute.

NOTE

4. On the File menu, click **Save**.

5. In the Save in drop–down list box, choose the **D:** drive. Your instructor will inform you if you need to save to an alternate location.

6. In the Save as type drop–down list box, choose **All Files**.

7. In the File name text box, enter **deleteAux*XX*.ldf** (where *XX* is the number of your server) and then click **Save**.

8. Close Notepad.

9. Click **Start** and then click **Command Prompt**.

10. Type **LDIFDE –I –S INSTRUCTOR.supercorp.net –f d:\deleteAux *XX*.ldf** (where *XX* is the number of your server) and press **Enter**. The file processing status is displayed, as shown in Figure 4-7. The Supercorp-Com-2004-manStaffInfo*XX* Auxiliary Class has been removed from the Supercorp-Com-2004-MAN-Staff-*XX* object's Auxiliary Class attribute.

```
Command Prompt                                              _|□|×|
Microsoft Windows [Version 5.2.3790]
(C) Copyright 1985-2003 Microsoft Corp.

C:\Documents and Settings\Administrator>LDIFDE -I -S INSTRUCTOR.supercorp.net -f
 d:\deleteAux01.ldf
Connecting to "INSTRUCTOR.supercorp.net"
Logging in as current user using SSPI
Importing directory from file "d:\deleteAux01.ldf"
Loading entries..
1 entry modified successfully.

The command has completed successfully

C:\Documents and Settings\Administrator>
```

Figure 4-7   Importing an LDIF file using LDIFDE

NOTE   Because the server holding the schema master of operations role is the only server from which you can modify the schema by default, you can use the *–S* option to specify the server holding the schema master role. In this example, INSTRUCTOR.supercorp.net is the schema master for the supercorp.net forest.

TIP   Type LDIFDE -? to view help on using the LDIFDE command.

11. Type **Exit** and press **Enter** to close the Command Prompt.

12. To locate additional information on the LDIF file format, you can view RFC 2849. To locate the RFC, click **Start**, select **All Programs**, and then click **Internet Explorer**.

13. If you receive a message box about Internet Explorer's Enhanced Security Configuration, check the box next to **In the future, do not show this message** and click **OK**.

14. In the Address bar, type **www.ietf.org/rfc/rfc2849.txt** and then click **Go**. If you wish, read the document.

NOTE   The LDIFDE utility does not support the "control:" keyword from RFC 2849.

15. When finished reviewing the RFC, close Internet Explorer.

16. After answering the review questions, log off your server.

Certification Objectives

Objectives for Microsoft Exam #70-294: Planning, Implementing, and Maintaining a Microsoft Windows Server 2003 Active Directory Infrastructure:

■ Implement an Active Directory directory service forest and domain structure.

■ Manage an Active Directory forest and domain structure.

■ Troubleshoot Active Directory.

4

REVIEW QUESTIONS

1. While you can use the –I parameter to import objects into Active Directory, which of the following LDIFDE parameters can you use to export objects from Active Directory?

   a. –E

   b. –O

   c. –U

   d. The absence of the -I parameter indicates you are performing an export.

2. You can use the _____ parameter of the LDIFDE command to enable verbose messages.

3. You can add the _____ character at the beginning of a line in an LDIF file to indicate that the line is a comment.

4. Which changetype can you specify to modify an object's relative distinguished name?

   a. rdnmod

   b. modrdn

   c. rdnch

   d. chrdn

5. You can create multiple objects using a single LDIF file. True or False?

Lab 4.5 Reloading the Schema Cache and Viewing Permissions

Objectives

The goal of this lab is to learn how to manually reload the schema cache. Additionally, you will also view the permissions that are set on the schema by default.

Materials Required

This lab will require the following:

- A Windows Server 2003 setup, as directed at the front of this lab manual

- A Microsoft Management Console with the Schema snap-in added and saved to the desktop

Estimated completion time: **5 minutes**

Activity Background

In order to improve performance on schema operations, such as validating a new object, every domain controller keeps a copy of the schema in memory, in addition to the copy stored on the hard disk. While the schema cache is automatically updated shortly after you update the schema, it may become necessary for you to manually reload the schema to see your modifications. You will learn how to manually reload the schema and view the default schema permissions in this lab.

Activity

1. If necessary, start your server and log on using the **AdminXX** account in the **CHILDXX** domain (where *XX* is the number of your server) using the password **Password01**.

2. On the desktop, double-click the **Schema console** you have already created that contains the Active Directory Schema snap-in.

3. Right-click the **Active Directory Schema** node in the left tree pane and then click **Reload the Schema**, as shown in Figure 4-8. This will reload the in-memory copy of the schema from the copy located on the hard disk.

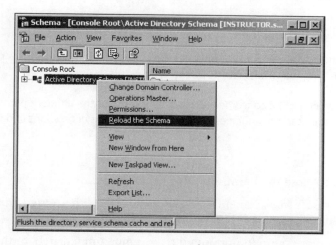

Figure 4-8   Reloading Active Directory Schema

4. Right-click the **Active Directory Schema** node in the left tree pane and then click **Permissions** to show the default permissions set on the schema, as shown in Figure 4-9.

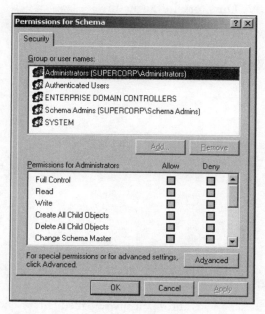

Figure 4-9   Default Active Directory Schema permissions

Because you are logged on with an account that does not have rights to modify the permissions set on the schema, most options will be disabled.

5. In the Group or user names list box, click **Schema Admins**.

6. In the Permissions for Schema Admins list box, review the permissions granted to members of the Schema Admins group by default.

For now, do not be concerned about the meaning of the different permissions or how they can be modified. Chapter 9 covers object permissions in detail.

7. Click **Cancel** to close the Permissions for Schema window.

8. Close the Microsoft Management Console that contains the Active Directory Schema snap-in. If prompted to save changes, click **No**.

9. Log off your server if you do not intend to continue immediately to the next project. Otherwise, stay logged on.

Certification Objectives

Objectives for Microsoft Exam #70-294: Planning, Implementing, and Maintaining a Microsoft Windows Server 2003 Active Directory Infrastructure:

■ Manage an Active Directory forest and domain structure.

■ Troubleshoot Active Directory.

REVIEW QUESTIONS

1. The members of which group can modify the schema by default?

   a. Forest Admins

   b. Schema Admins

   c. Structure Admins

   d. Enterprise Admins

2. The schema _____ is an in-memory copy of the schema that is used to improve validation performance.

3. The in-memory copy of the schema is automatically reloaded (after a short delay) each time you make a modification. True or False?

4. Members of Schema Admins are granted permission to Delete All Child Objects. True or False?

5. Which account is automatically made a member of the Schema Admins group?

   a. The built-in Administrator account from the forest root domain

   b. The built-in Administrator account from the root of each tree in the forest

   c. The built-in Administrator account from every domain

   d. The built-in Enterprise Admin account from every domain

4

LAB 4.6 LOCATING THE GUIDE TO SECURING THE SCHEMA

Objectives

The goal of this lab is to locate the guide to securing the schema provided by the United States National Security Agency.

Materials Required

This lab will require the following:

- A Windows Server 2003 setup, as directed at the front of this lab manual

- A connection to the Internet

Estimated completion time:**15 minutes**

Activity Background

The United States National Security Agency provides many documents containing security best practices. In this lab, you will locate a guide to securing the schema. Keep in mind that you can also locate many other security guides by following these steps.

ACTIVITY

Activity

1. If necessary, start your server and log on using the **AdminXX** account in the **CHILDXX** domain (where XX is the number of your server) using the password **Password01**.

   NOTE
   Before you can view the guide to securing the schema, you must first have Adobe Reader installed. If your instructor has already installed Adobe Reader or downloaded the Adobe Reader setup files, follow the instructions given by your instructor and then continue at step 12.

2. Click **Start**, select **All Programs**, and then click **Internet Explorer**.

3. In the Address bar, type **www.adobe.com/reader** and then click **Go**.

4. Towards the bottom of the page, click the **text-only Adobe Reader download page** link.

5. Click the **Adobe Reader 6.0, full version** link.

6. Click the **Adobe Reader 6.0 — English for Windows, 16MB** link.

7. When prompted to save or open the file, click **Open**.

8. Once the download completes, click **Yes** on the Security Warning screen.

9. Once the Installation wizard starts, click **Next** on all screens (you may need to click Next multiple times) to use all the default options. Then click the **Install** button on the final screen.

10. Once the installation has completed, click **Finish** to close the wizard. You must now restart Internet Explorer.

11. Close **Internet Explorer**.

12. Click **Start**, select **All Programs**, and then click **Internet Explorer**.

13. In the Address bar of Internet Explorer, type **nsa2.www.conxion.com/win2k/download.htm** and then click **Go**.

14. If a legal notice appears, review the notice and then click **OK** to continue.

Although the document was written for Windows 2000, the security recommendations contained within the document are still applicable to Windows 2003.

NOTE

15. Click the link **Guide to Securing Microsoft Windows 2000 Schema** (you will need to scroll down).

16. If this is the first time you are using Adobe Reader, you will need to click **Accept** on the licensing agreement. Note that this agreement has to do with the Adobe Reader software and not the United States National Security Agency Web site.

You may need to minimize Internet Explorer to see the licensing agreement. If Internet Explorer shows a blank white screen after clicking the *Guide to Securing Microsoft Windows 2000 Schema* link, minimize Internet Explorer.

CAUTION

17. If you wish, read the document.

18. After answering the review questions, close Internet Explorer.

19. After answering the review questions, log off your server.

REVIEW QUESTIONS

1. Schema modifications cannot be undone. True or False?

2. Before you modify the schema, you should perform a complete _____ of your system.

3. The schema is the _____ for Active Directory, containing the definition for the universe of objects that can be stored in the directory.

4. An Active Directory forest contains how many schemas?

    a. One for the entire forest

    b. One for each tree in the forest

    c. One for each domain in the forest

    d. One for each organizational unit

5. It is not possible for third-party applications to modify the schema. All schema modifications must be done manually. True or False?

ACTIVE DIRECTORY LOGICAL DESIGN

Labs included in this chapter:

◆ Lab 5.1 Verifying a Trust Relationship

◆ Lab 5.2 Examining Default Containers and Organizational Units

◆ Lab 5.3 Renaming and Reorganizing Organizational Units

◆ Lab 5.4 Working with Organizational Units by Using Command Line Tools

◆ Lab 5.5 Locating Information on Unattended Promotion and Demotion of Domain Controllers

Microsoft MCSE Exam #70-294 Objectives	
Objective	Lab
Implement an Active Directory directory service forest and domain structure.	5.1, 5.5
Manage an Active Directory forest and domain structure.	5.1, 5.5
Implement an OU structure.	5.2, 5.3, 5.4

LAB 5.1 VERIFYING A TRUST RELATIONSHIP

Objectives

The goal of this lab is to learn how an existing trust relationship can be verified using Active Directory Domains and Trusts.

Materials Required

This lab will require the following:

- A Windows Server 2003 setup, as directed at the front of this lab manual

Estimated completion time: **10 minutes**

Activity Background

A trust relationship is based on a password that is only known by the trusted and trusting domains. For security reasons, every seven days a new password is chosen and the previous password is also stored (in case a crash occurs just after the passwords are changed on one end). In other words, this means a trust password is valid for up to 14 days. If two domains are unable to communicate with each other for an extended period of time, it is possible for the passwords used by the trusted and trusting domains to be out of sync. In this lab, you will learn how to use Active Directory Domains and Trusts to verify that a trust is working correctly—which includes a check to be sure that the passwords are in sync. Note that Chapter 14 covers how to verify and reset a trust relationship using NETDOM.

Activity

1. If necessary, start your server and log on using the **Administrator** account in the **CHILDXX** domain (where *XX* is the number of the forest root domain for which your server is a domain controller) using the password **Password01**.

2. Click **Start**, select **Administrative Tools**, and then click **Active Directory Domains and Trusts**.

While Active Directory Domains and Trusts provides a graphical way of verifying trust relationships, you can also use the NETDOM and NETDIAG command-line tools included in the Windows Server 2003 support tools to verify trust relationships.

3. In the left tree pane, right-click **childXX.supercorp.net** (where *XX* is the number of the forest root domain for which your server is a domain controller) and then click **Properties**.

4. Click the **Trusts** tab.

5. In the Domains trusted by this domain (outgoing trusts) list box, click **supercorp.net**, as shown in Figure 5-1.

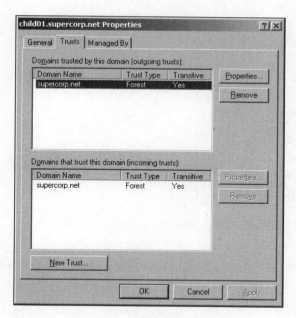

Figure 5-1   Selecting a trust to verify

6. Click **Properties**.

7. On the General tab of supercorp.net Properties, click **Validate**.

8. When prompted if you would like to validate the incoming trust, click the **Yes, validate the incoming trust** option button. This will allow you to verify both directions of the two-way trust.

9. You must enter the credentials for a user account that has administrative rights in the trusting domain. Enter **Administrator** in the User name drop-down list box and **Password01** in the Password text box, as shown in Figure 5-2.

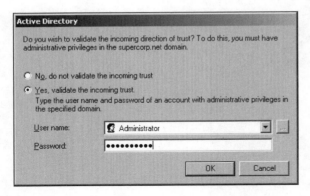

Figure 5-2   Entering credentials for the trusting domain

10. Click **OK**. A message box will state if the trust was correctly verified or not.

11. Click **OK**.

12. If prompted to update the name suffix routing information, click **No**. (Name Suffixes are used in forest trusts to determine in which forest a user account is located.)

13. On the supercorp.net Properties window, note the information located on each of the tabs and then click **Cancel** to discard any changes you may have made inadvertently.

14. Click **Cancel** to close the child*XX*.supercorp.net Properties window.

15. Close Active Directory Domains and Trusts.

16. Log off your server if you do not intend to continue immediately to the next project. Otherwise, stay logged on.

Certification Objectives

Objectives for Microsoft Exam #70-294: Planning, Implementing, and Maintaining a Microsoft Windows Server 2003 Active Directory Infrastructure:

■ Implement an Active Directory directory service forest and domain structure.

■ Manage an Active Directory forest and domain structure.

REVIEW QUESTIONS

1. A _____ gives a user in one domain the ability to access a resource in another, without needing separate credentials for each domain.

2. Trust _____ determines if the trust extends outside the two domains in which the trust is formed.

3. A trust relationship is automatically established between which domains in a forest?

   a. Every domain in a forest has a trust relationship with every other domain in the same forest.

   b. Every domain in a forest has a trust relationship with the root domain of the forest.

   c. Child domains have a trust relationship with their parent domain, and the root of each tree has a trust relationship with the root of the forest.

   d. Domains in a forest do not have any trusts automatically created; they must all be added manually.

4. The term _____ means that domain A trusts domain B, and domain B trusts domain A.

5. In a _____ trust, the trust between two domains does not extend outside those two domains.

5

LAB 5.2 EXAMINING DEFAULT CONTAINERS AND ORGANIZATIONAL UNITS

Objectives

The goal of this lab is to learn what containers and organizational units exist in a newly created Active Directory installation. You will also learn the differences between containers and organizational units.

Materials Required

This lab will require the following:

- A Windows Server 2003 setup, as directed at the front of this lab manual

Estimated completion time: **10 minutes**

Activity Background

There are several default containers and organizational units created when you install Active Directory. This lab will familiarize you with these default objects and will also help you become more comfortable with Active Directory Users and Computers.

ACTIVITY

Activity

1. If necessary, start your server and log on using the **Administrator** account in the **CHILDXX** domain (where *XX* is the number of the forest root domain for which your server is a domain controller) using the password **Password01**.

2. Click **Start**, select **Administrative Tools**, and then click **Active Directory Users and Computers**.

3. In the left tree pane, expand **childXX.supercorp.net** (where *XX* is the number of the forest root domain for which your server is a domain controller) if necessary.

4. Note the default containers and organizational units. Keep in mind that the North America *XX* (where *XX* is the number of your server and your partner's server) organizational unit(s) were created in a Chapter 5 main text activity and are not created by default.

5. Click the **Users** container in the left tree pane. The container contents will be displayed in the right details pane. Note the types of objects contained in this container by default.

6. Click the **Domain Controllers** organizational unit in the left tree pane. The organizational unit contents will display in the right details pane. Note that the icon for an organizational unit contains a folder graphic on the folder; icons for containers do not.

7. Right-click the **Users** container and then click **Properties**. The Users container properties will appear, as shown in Figure 5-3. Note the available information, and then click **Cancel** to discard changes you may have made inadvertently.

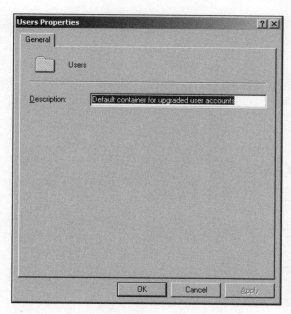

Figure 5-3   Users container properties

5

8. Right-click the **Domain Controllers** organizational unit and then click **Properties**. The Domain Controllers organizational unit properties will display, as shown in Figure 5-4.

Figure 5-4   Domain Controllers organizational unit Properties

9. Note the available information on each tab and examples of information/features available for organizational units that are not available with containers. When finished, click **Cancel** to discard any changes you may have made inadvertently.

10. On the View menu, click **Advanced Features**. Note the additional containers that appear directly under the child*XX*.supercorp.net object in the left tree pane.

11. Right-click the **Domain Controllers** organizational unit and then click **Properties**. Note the additional tabs that appear, and the type of information found on each.

12. When finished, click **Cancel** to discard any changes you may have made.

13. After answering the review questions, close Active Directory Users and Computers.

14. Log off your server if you do not intend to continue immediately to the next project. Otherwise, stay logged on.

Certification Objectives

Objectives for Microsoft Exam #70-294: Planning, Implementing, and Maintaining a Microsoft Windows Server 2003 Active Directory Infrastructure:

- Implement an OU structure.

REVIEW QUESTIONS

1. You can use the _____ tab located in the properties of an organizational unit to identify the object class of an object.

2. Unlike _____, _____ have a tab for linking Group Policy Objects to them.

3. If you are unable to locate the Security tab when viewing a container's properties, you most likely need to do which of the following?

   a. Enable Advanced View on the View menu.

   b. Enable Advanced Features on the View menu.

   c. Enable Advanced Features on the File menu.

   d. Nothing, containers do not have a Security tab

4. The computer accounts for domain controllers are created in the _____ organizational unit, by default.

5. For Active Directory integrated DNS zones stored in the domain partition, where can you locate the objects that make up the zone using Active Directory Users and Computers?

   a. System > MicrosoftDNS

   b. System > DNS

   c. Program Data > MicrosoftDNS

   d. Program Data > Microsoft

LAB 5.3 RENAMING AND REORGANIZING ORGANIZATIONAL UNITS

Objectives

The goal of this lab is to learn how to move, rename, and delete organizational units.

Materials Required

This lab will require the following:

- A Windows Server 2003 setup, as directed at the front of this lab manual

Estimated completion time: **10 minutes**

Activity Background

While forests and domains are not easily modified, organizational units can be created, deleted, moved, or renamed with little effort. In this lab, you will learn how to perform common administrative tasks related to organizational units, such as moving and renaming them from Active Directory Users and Computers.

Activity

1. If necessary, start your server and log on using the **Administrator** account in the **CHILDXX** domain (where *XX* is the number of the forest root domain for which your server is a domain controller) using the password **Password01**.

2. Click **Start**, select **Administrative Tools**, and then click **Active Directory Users and Computers**.

3. If necessary, on the View menu, click **Advanced Features** to turn off the display of Advanced Features.

4. Right-click **childXX.supercorp.net** (where *XX* is the number of the forest root domain for which your server is a domain controller), select **New**, and then click **Organizational Unit**.

5. In the Name text box, enter **Temp Location XX** (where *XX* is the number of your server) and then click **OK**.

6. Repeat Steps 4 and 5 to create an additional organizational unit named **Temp Sub Location XX** (where *XX* is the number of your server), as shown in Figure 5-5.

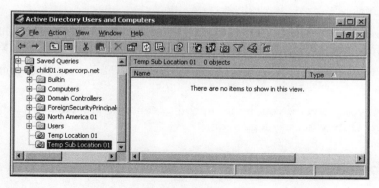

Figure 5-5   New organizational units

7. Right-click **Temp Sub Location XX** (where *XX* is the number of your server) and then click **Move**.

8. In the Move window, select **Temp Location XX** (where *XX* is the number of your server) and then click **OK**.

9. In the left tree pane, double-click **Temp Location XX** (where *XX* is the number of your server) to expand the node and show its details in the right pane. Note that Temp Sub Location *XX* has been moved within this organizational unit.

10. Right-click **Temp Sub Location XX** (where *XX* is the number of your server) and click **Rename**.

11. The text for the organizational unit name should become editable. Type **Sales** and then press **Enter**. Your screen should look similar to Figure 5-6.

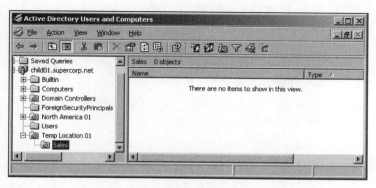

Figure 5-6   Renamed organizational unit

12. Right-click **Temp Location XX** (where *XX* is the number of your server) and then click **Delete**.

13. A message box will prompt you to confirm that you want to delete the object. Click **Yes**.

14. Because you are deleting an object that contains other objects, you will be prompted again to confirm that you want to delete the object. Click **Yes**.

15. After answering the review questions, close Active Directory Users and Computers.

16. Log off your server if you do not intend to continue immediately to the next project. Otherwise, stay logged on.

Certification Objectives

Objectives for Microsoft Exam #70-294: Planning, Implementing, and Maintaining a Microsoft Windows Server 2003 Active Directory Infrastructure:

- Implement an OU structure.

REVIEW QUESTIONS

1. Which menu at the top of Active Directory Users and Computers can you use to view the same menu that is available when right-clicking an object?

   a. File

   b. Action

   c. View

   d. Window

2. If you attempt to move an organizational unit into a container, such as the Users container, what will happen?

   a. The move operation will complete successfully.

   b. The move operation will complete, but the organizational unit will be converted to a container.

   c. The move operation will complete, but the container will be converted to an organizational unit.

   d. You will receive an error that the parent object to which you are trying to move the object is not listed as a possible superior.

3. It is possible to move an organizational unit that contains nested organizational units. True or False?

4. Unlike domains and forests, _____ can be reorganized without much difficulty.

5. In Active Directory Users and Computers, _____ cannot be created, moved, renamed, or deleted.

LAB 5.4 WORKING WITH ORGANIZATIONAL UNITS BY USING COMMAND-LINE TOOLS

5

Objectives

The goal of this lab is to learn about the command-line tools available to work with organizational units.

Materials Required

This lab will require the following:

- A Windows Server 2003 setup, as directed at the front of this lab manual

Estimated completion time: **15 minutes**

Activity Background

In Chapter 1, you learned about two of the new command-line tools: dsquery and dsget. In this lab, you will learn how to use three more of the command-line tools that are available: dsadd, dsmove, and dsrm. While this lab explicitly looks at using these commands to work with organizational units, keep in mind that these commands can also be used to work with a variety of other directory objects, such as users and groups.

ACTIVITY

Activity

1. If necessary, start your server and log on using the **Administrator** account in the **CHILDXX** domain (where *XX* is the number of the forest root domain for which your server is a domain controller) using the password **Password01**.

2. Click **Start** and then click **Command Prompt**.

3. Type **DSQUERY OU** and press **Enter**. A list of organizational units contained in the domain is displayed.

4. Type **DSADD OU "OU=Command XX,DC=childZZ,DC=supercorp, DC=net"** (where *XX* is the number of your server and *ZZ* is the number of the forest root domain for which your server is a domain controller) and press **Enter**.

TIP   The quotation marks around the Distinguished Name are required because the name contains spaces.

5. Repeat Step 4 to create two additional organizational units with the following distinguished names (where *XX* is the number of your server and *ZZ* is the number of the forest root domain for which your server is a domain controller). Your screen should look similar to Figure 5-7.

OU=Sub 1 Command *XX*,DC=child*ZZ*,DC=supercorp,DC=net

OU=Sub 2 Command *XX*,OU=Command *XX*,DC=child*ZZ*,DC=super-corp,DC=net

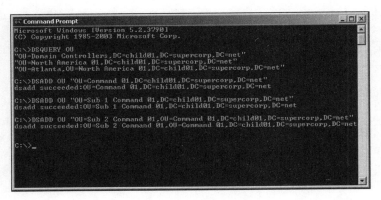

Figure 5-7   Creating new organizational units using DSADD

NOTE   Your command prompt is most likely not going to C:\> by default (as shown in Figure 5-7), but rather C:\Documents and Settings\Administrator.SERVER*XX*> (where *XX* is the number of your server). It could even be something else, depending on your server's configuration. The command prompt has been changed in the rest of this text's figures to keep commands from wrapping to the next line as much as possible. Unless noted otherwise, the prompt you execute the commands at does not matter. If you would like to change your start menu's Command Prompt shortcut to start the prompt at C:\>, you can do so by clicking Start, right-clicking Command Prompt, and then clicking Properties. Change the Start in the textbox to C:\, or any path you like, and then click OK. The next time you click the Command Prompt shortcut, the prompt will start in the directory you specify.

6. Type **DSMOVE "OU=Sub 1 Command XX,DC=childZZ,DC=supercorp, DC=net"-newparent "OU=Command XX,DC=childZZ,DC=supercorp, DC=net"** (where *XX* is the number of your server and *ZZ* is the number of the forest root domain for which your server is a domain controller) and press **Enter**. The *Sub 1 Command XX* organizational unit is moved to the *Command XX* organizational unit.

7. Click **Start**, select **Administrative Tools**, and then click **Active Directory Users and Computers**.

8. Expand the necessary objects in the left tree pane to locate the organizational units you have created using DSADD, as shown in Figure 5-8.

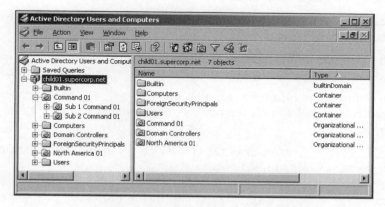

Figure 5-8   Viewing newly created organizational units in Active Directory Users and Computers

9. Close Active Directory Users and Computers.

10. At the Command Prompt window you already have open, type **DSRM –subtree "OU=Command XX,DC=childZZ, DC=supercorp,DC=net"** (where *XX* is the number of your server and *ZZ* is the number of the forest root domain for which your server is a domain controller) and press **Enter**.

11. When prompted if you are sure you wish to delete the object, type **Y** and press **Enter**.

12. Type **DSQUERY OU** and press **Enter** to see that the organizational units you created have been removed.

13. After answering the review questions, type **Exit** and press **Enter** to close the Command Prompt window.

14. Log off your server if you do not intend to continue immediately to the next project. Otherwise, stay logged on.

5

Certification Objectives

Objectives for Microsoft Exam #70-294: Planning, Implementing, and Maintaining a Microsoft Windows Server 2003 Active Directory Infrastructure:

- Implement an OU structure.

REVIEW QUESTIONS

1. You can use the _____ command to create new objects including users, groups, and organizational units.

2. You can use the _____ command to relocate objects including users, groups, and organizational units.

3. When removing an organizational unit, the _____ parameter specifies that you want to delete the object and all the objects under the specified object.

4. When removing an organizational unit, the _____ parameter specifies that you want to delete only the objects under the specified object (but not the object itself).

5. The _____ parameter of the DSMOVE command lets you change an object's relative Distinguished Name.

LAB 5.5 LOCATING INFORMATION ON UNATTENDED PROMOTION AND DEMOTION OF DOMAIN CONTROLLERS

Objectives

The goal of this lab is to locate information on creating unattended answer files that you can use to promote and demote both Windows 2000 Server and Windows Server 2003 domain controllers.

Materials Required

This lab will require the following:

- A Windows Server 2003 setup, as directed at the front of this lab manual

- A connection to the Internet

Estimated completion time: **10 minutes**

Activity Background

When only a small number of domain controllers need to be promoted, manually using DCPROMO to promote the domain controllers is straightforward. However, when you have dozens of domain controllers, or technical staff that are unfamiliar with the promotion process, creating an unattended answer file can be extremely useful. In this lab, you will learn how to locate the documentation needed to create an unattended answer file from Microsoft's support Web site.

Activity

1. If necessary, start your server and log on using the **Administrator** account in the **CHILDXX** domain (where *XX* is the number of the forest root domain for which your server is a domain controller) using the password **Password01**.

2. Click **Start**, select **All Programs**, and then click **Internet Explorer**.

3. If you are prompted about Internet Explorer's enhanced security configuration, check the box next to **In the future, do not show this message** and click **OK**.

4. On the Tools menu, click **Internet Options**.

5. On the Security tab, check to see if the security level slider is set to **Medium** for the Internet zone. If it is not, move the slider so the security level is set to Medium. Click **Yes** if you are prompted to confirm that you want to change the level.

If a slider does not appear, you may need to click the "Default Level" button. You can then move the slider from High to Medium.

6. Click **OK**.

7. In the address bar, type **support.microsoft.com** and click **Go**.

8. On the left side menu, under "Search the Knowledge Base," type **Unattended Promotion and Demotion of Domain Controllers** and then press **Enter**.

Microsoft's Web site is often reorganized. The search area may have been moved to another location on the support Web page.

9. If warned that you are sending information to the Internet, click **Yes**.

10. Click the link titled **Unattended Promotion and Demotion of Windows 2000 Domain Controllers** (article number 223757).

NOTE You can use the Notepad application, located under Start, All Programs, Accessories, to write custom answer files.

11. If you wish, read the document.

12. After answering the review questions, close Internet Explorer.

13. Log off your server.

Certification Objectives

Objectives for Microsoft Exam #70-294: Planning, Implementing, and Maintaining a Microsoft Windows Server 2003 Active Directory Infrastructure:

- Implement an Active Directory directory service forest and domain structure.

- Manage an Active Directory forest and domain structure.

REVIEW QUESTIONS

1. Which of the following commands could you run in order to start an unattended promotion of a domain controller using an answer file named answer.txt located on the A: drive?

   a. DCPROMO /unattend:A:\answer.txt

   b. DCPROMO /answer:A:\answer.txt

   c. DCPROMO /dsinstall:A:\answer.txt

   d. PROMOTE /unattend:A:\answer.txt

2. Use the _____ field to specify the DNS name of a new forest or tree.

3. Use the _____ field to specify the location in which to store the active directory database.

4. Use the _____ field to specify the NetBIOS name of a new domain.

5. Use the _____ field to specify if this is the last domain controller in a domain when demoting a domain controller.

6

ACTIVE DIRECTORY PHYSICAL DESIGN

Labs included in this chapter:

♦ Lab 6.1 Testing IP Connectivity

♦ Lab 6.2 Determining if the "Bridge all site links" Option Is Enabled

♦ Lab 6.3 Creating and Modifying Site Link Bridges

♦ Lab 6.4 Working with Subnets

♦ Lab 6.5 Enabling Universal Group Caching

♦ Lab 6.6 Identifying Replication Partners

Microsoft MCSE Exam #70-294 Objectives	
Objective	Lab
Implement an Active Directory directory service forest and domain structure.	6.5
Implement an Active Directory site topology.	6.1, 6.2, 6.3, 6.4
Monitor Active Directory replication failures.	6.6

LAB 6.1 TESTING IP CONNECTIVITY

Objectives

The goal of this lab is to learn how you can use the Ping and Tracert commands to test IP connectivity between sites.

Materials Required

This lab will require the following:

- A Windows Server 2003 setup, as directed at the front of this lab manual

Estimated completion time:**5 minutes**

Activity Background

The Ping and Tracert commands are invaluable for testing network connectivity between two hosts on a TCP/IP-based network. When mapping out your network, you can also use these commands to learn more about the network topology. In this activity, you will learn how to use the Ping and Tracert commands.

ACTIVITY

Activity

1. If necessary, start your server and log on using the **Administrator** account in the **CHILDXX** domain (where *XX* is the number of the forest root domain for which your server is a domain controller) using the password **Password01**.

2. Click **Start** and then click **Command Prompt**.

3. Type **PING SERVERXX** (where *XX* is the number of your partner's server) and then press **Enter**. If your partner's server is on, you should receive results similar to those shown in Figure 6-1. If you receive a "Request timed out" error, you do not have IP connectivity with the remote server.

```
Command Prompt                                                    _ □ ×
Microsoft Windows [Version 5.2.3790]
<C> Copyright 1985-2003 Microsoft Corp.

C:\>PING SERVER02

Pinging SERVER02.child01.supercorp.net [192.168.1.2] with 32 bytes of data:

Reply from 192.168.1.2: bytes=32 time=6ms TTL=128
Reply from 192.168.1.2: bytes=32 time<1ms TTL=128
Reply from 192.168.1.2: bytes=32 time<1ms TTL=128
Reply from 192.168.1.2: bytes=32 time<1ms TTL=128

Ping statistics for 192.168.1.2:
    Packets: Sent = 4, Received = 4, Lost = 0 <0% loss>,
Approximate round trip times in milli-seconds:
    Minimum = 0ms, Maximum = 6ms, Average = 1ms

C:\>_
```

Figure 6-1   Replies from remote server

4. Type **TRACERT SERVERXX** (where *XX* is the number of your partner's server) and then press **Enter**.

5. Because your server and your partner's server are most likely on the same network, you will only see one hop. To get a better idea of what the TRACERT command does, type **TRACERT www.microsoft.com** and then press **Enter**. The path that data takes from your server to Microsoft's Web server is displayed.

NOTE   If the TRACERT command does not fully complete (i.e., it stops after a few hops) when attempting to trace the path to *www.microsoft.com* you are most likely behind a firewall that blocks ICMP traffic. You can hold down the Ctrl key and then press C to stop the trace if this occurs.

6. Type **EXIT** and then press **Enter**.

7. Log off your server if you do not intend to continue immediately to the next project. Otherwise, stay logged on.

Certification Objectives

Objectives for Microsoft Exam #70-294: Planning, Implementing, and Maintaining a Microsoft Windows Server 2003 Active Directory Infrastructure:

- Implement an Active Directory site topology.

REVIEW QUESTIONS

1. You can use the _____ command to determine if IP connectivity exists between two hosts.

2. You can use the _____ command to trace the route that data would take between two hosts.

3. When using the Ping command, the _____ error indicates that the remote host could not be contacted.

4. You can use the _____ parameter of the Ping command to ping the specified host until Ctrl+Break or Crtl+C is pressed. (Use the ping –? command if you are unsure.)

5. When using the Tracert command, if only one hop is shown this means which of the following?

   a. The remote host is on the same network.

   b. The remote host is on a different network that is directly connected.

   c. The remote host is not reachable.

   d. One hop does not indicate any information.

LAB 6.2 DETERMINING IF THE "BRIDGE ALL SITE LINKS" OPTION IS ENABLED

Objectives

The goal of this lab is to locate the "Bridge all site links" option, so that you will be able to identify the status of the option and change it if necessary.

Materials Required

This lab will require the following:

- A Windows Server 2003 setup, as directed at the front of this lab manual

Estimated completion time: **5 minutes**

Activity Background

By default, Active Directory assumes that a fully routed IP infrastructure is in place. In a fully routed IP environment, devices in one site can communicate with the devices in all other sites. In this activity, you will locate the settings in Active Directory Users and Computers that control whether Active Directory assumes a fully routed IP infrastructure is in place or not.

Activity

1. If necessary, start your server and log on using the **Administrator** account in the **CHILDXX** domain (where *XX* is the number of the forest root domain for which your server is a domain controller) using the password **Password01**.

2. Click **Start**, select **Administrative Tools**, and then click **Active Directory Sites and Services**.

3. If necessary, in the left tree pane, expand the **Sites** folder.

4. In the left tree pane, expand the **Inter–Site Transports** folder.

5. In the left tree pane, right-click the **IP** folder and then click **Properties**. This will display the IP transport properties as shown in Figure 6-2.

6

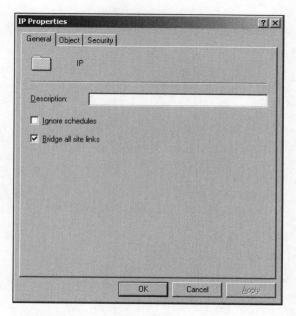

Figure 6-2   IP Properties

6. Note the status of the **Bridge all site links** check box, and then click **Cancel** to discard any accidental changes that you may have made.

7. In the left tree pane, right-click the **SMTP** folder and then click **Properties**.

8. Note the status of the **Bridge all site links** check box, and then click **Cancel** to discard any accidental changes that you may have made.

9. Close Active Directory Sites and Services.

10. Log off your server if you do not intend to continue immediately to the next project. Otherwise, stay logged on.

Certification Objectives

Objectives for Microsoft Exam #70-294: Planning, Implementing, and Maintaining a Microsoft Windows Server 2003 Active Directory Infrastructure:

- Implement an Active Directory site topology.

Review Questions

1. When the IP environment is not _____, you should disable the "Bridge all site links" option and manually create site link bridges.

2. Which of the following tools do you use to modify automatic bridging of site links?

    a. Active Directory Domains and Trusts

    b. Active Directory Sites and Services

    c. Active Directory Users and Computers

    d. Active Directory Schema

3. There are two "Bridge all site links" options, one for the _____ transport protocol and another for the _____ transport protocol.

4. The "Bridge all site links" option is _____ for all transport protocols by default.

    a. enabled

    b. disabled

    c. It depends on the domain functional level.

    d. It depends on the forest functional level.

5. Both SMTP and IP are examples of _____ protocols.

    a. intrasite transport

    b. intersite transport

    c. intradomain transport

    d. intradomain authentication

LAB 6.3 CREATING AND MODIFYING SITE LINK BRIDGES

Objectives

The goal of this lab is to familiarize you with the process of creating and modifying site link bridges.

Materials Required

This lab will require the following:

- A Windows Server 2003 setup, as directed at the front of this lab manual

6

Estimated completion time: **10 minutes**

Activity Background

If you do not have a fully routed IP infrastructure in place, you will need to disable the Bridge all site links option for the appropriate transport protocol(s) and create site link bridges. Site link bridges indicate to Active Directory which site links have connectivity with each other. In this activity, you will learn how to create a site link bridge.

Activity

1. If necessary, start your server and log on using the **Administrator** account in the **CHILDXX** domain (where *XX* is the number of the forest root domain for which your server is a domain controller) using the password **Password01**.

2. Click **Start**, select **Administrative Tools**, and then click **Active Directory Sites and Services**.

3. If necessary, in the left tree pane, expand the **Sites** folder.

4. In the left tree pane, expand the **Inter-Site Transports** folder.

5. Right-click the **IP** folder and then click **New Site Link Bridge**.

6. In the Name text box, type **MyBridgeXX** (where *XX* is the number of your server).

7. If necessary, use the **Add** or **Remove** buttons to ensure that **DEFAULTIPSITELINK** and **MyLinkXX** (where *XX* is the number of your server) are the only site links that are part of this bridge, as shown in Figure 6-3.

Figure 6-3   Creating a site link bridge

8. Click **OK** to create the new bridge.

9. In the left tree pane, click the **IP** folder to display in the right details pane a list of site links and site link bridges that have been created.

10. In the right pane, right-click **MyBridgeXX** (where *XX* is the number of your server) and then click **Properties** to display its properties.

11. In the Description text box, type **Test Bridge** and then click **OK**.

12. In the right pane, right-click **MyBridgeXX** (where *XX* is the number of your server) and then click **Rename**.

13. Type **MyTestBridgeXX** (where *XX* is the number of your server) and then press **Enter**. The bridge is renamed, as shown in Figure 6-4.

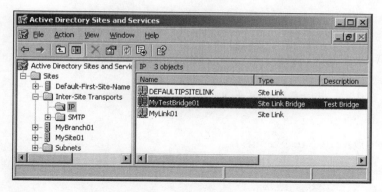

Figure 6-4 Renaming a site link bridge

14. In the right pane, right-click **MyTestBridgeXX** (where *XX* is the number of your server) and then click **Delete**.

15. When prompted to confirm that you want to delete the object, click **Yes**.

16. Close Active Directory Sites and Services.

17. Log off your server if you do not intend to continue immediately to the next project. Otherwise, stay logged on.

Certification Objectives

Objectives for Microsoft Exam #70-294: Planning, Implementing, and Maintaining a Microsoft Windows Server 2003 Active Directory Infrastructure:

■ Implement an Active Directory site topology.

REVIEW QUESTIONS

1. Which of the following are added to a site link bridge?

    a. sites

    b. site links

    c. subnets

    d. other site link bridges

2. Like site links, site link bridges have a configurable cost. True or False?

3. How many site links does Active Directory Sites and Services define by default?

   a. 0

   b. 1

   c. 2

   d. 3

4. What is the name of the site that Active Directory creates by default?

   a. First-Default-Site

   b. First-Default-Site-Name

   c. Default-First-Site

   d. Default-First-Site-Name

5. Site link bridges cannot be created using site links that use the SMTP inter-site transport protocol. True or False?

LAB 6.4 WORKING WITH SUBNETS

Objectives

The goal of this lab is to learn how to work with subnets.

Materials Required

This lab will require the following:

- A Windows Server 2003 setup, as directed at the front of this lab manual

Estimated completion time: **10 minutes**

Activity Background

A site is made up of one or more well-connected IP subnets. In order to define which subnets make up a given site, you must create subnet objects. In this activity, you will learn how to work with subnet objects.

Activity

1. If necessary, start your server and log on using the **Administrator** account in the **CHILDXX** domain (where XX is the number of the forest root domain for which your server is a domain controller) using the password **Password01**.

2. Click **Start**, select **Administrative Tools**, and then click **Active Directory Sites and Services**.

3. If necessary, in the left tree pane, expand the **Sites** folder.

4. In the left tree pane, right–click **Subnets** and then click **New Subnet**.

5. In the Address text box, enter **192.168.100.0**.

6. In the Mask text box, enter **255.255.255.0**.

7. Select **MySiteXX** (where *XX* is the number of your server) from the list of sites, as shown in Figure 6-5.

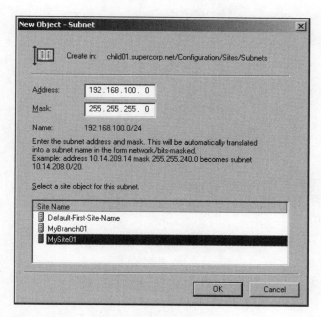

Figure 6-5   Creating a new subnet

8. Click **OK**.

9. If necessary, expand the **Subnets** folder in the left tree pane.

10. In the left tree pane, right–click **192.168.100.0/24** and then click **Properties**.

11. In the Description text box, enter **Florida Branch Office**.

12. In the Site drop-down list box, select **MyBranch01**, as shown in Figure 6-6.

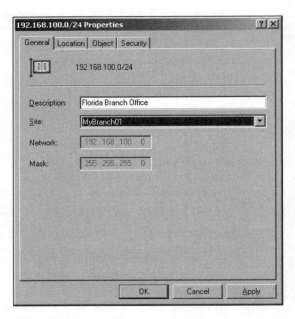

Figure 6-6   Modifying a subnet

13. Click **OK**.

14. In the left tree pane, click **Subnets** to show a list of subnets in the right details pane.

15. Right-click **Subnets** in the left tree pane and then click **Export List**.

16. In the Save in drop-down list box, ensure that **My Documents** is selected.

17. In the File name drop-down combo box, enter **List of sites**.

18. Click **Save**.

19. Close Active Directory Sites and Services.

20. Click **Start** and then click **Windows Explorer**.

21. The Windows Explorer window should open directly to your My Documents folder. If not, select **My Documents** in the left tree pane.

22. Open the List of sites file and review the information contained in the file.

23. Close the List of sites file and then close Windows Explorer.

24. Log off your server if you do not intend to continue immediately to the next project. Otherwise, stay logged on.

Certification Objectives

Objectives for Microsoft Exam #70-294: Planning, Implementing, and Maintaining a Microsoft Windows Server 2003 Active Directory Infrastructure:

- Implement an Active Directory site topology.

REVIEW QUESTIONS

6

1. Which of the following tools do you use to define subnet objects in Active Directory?

   a. Active Directory Domains and Trusts

   b. Active Directory Sites and Services

   c. Active Directory Users and Computers

   d. Services

2. How many sites can an Active Directory subnet be associated with?

   a. 0

   b. 1

   c. 2

   d. 3

3. Which of the following pieces of information must be entered in the New Subnet dialog box when defining a new subnet in Active Directory Sites and Services? (Choose all that apply.)

   a. subnet IP address

   b. subnet mask

   c. domain name

   d. site name

4. The subnet represented by the address 192.168.16.0 and subnet mask 255.255.240.0 can also be represented as 192.168.16.0/_____.

5. What subnet mask would be associated with the 192.168.24.0/23 subnet?

   a. 255.255.254.0

   b. 255.255.224.0

   c. 255.255.248.0

   d. 255.255.255.0

Lab 6.5 Enabling Universal Group Caching

Objectives

The goal of this lab is to learn how to enable universal group caching for a site.

Materials Required

This lab will require the following:

- A Windows Server 2003 setup, as directed at the front of this lab manual

Estimated completion time: **5 minutes**

Activity Background

When a site contains one or more domain controllers, but no global catalog servers, universal group caching should typically be enabled for the site. When universal group caching is enabled, the first time a user logs on, a domain controller in the local site retrieves the user's universal group membership from a global catalog server. The domain controller in the local site then caches the user's universal group membership for use in subsequent logons. The next time the user logs on, the domain controller in the local site uses the cached information instead of contacting a global catalog server. This can speed up the logon process—a global catalog server from another site does not have to be contacted over a slow WAN link to retrieve the user's universal group membership. Note that the cached universal group information is automatically refreshed from a global catalog server every eight hours by default. Additionally, once a user's universal group membership is cached, it is cached indefinitely.

Activity

1. If necessary, start your server and log on using the **Administrator** account in the **CHILDXX** domain (where *XX* is the number of the forest root domain for which your server is a domain controller) using the password **Password01**.

2. Click **Start**, select **Administrative Tools**, and then click **Active Directory Sites and Services**.

3. If necessary, in the left tree pane, expand the Sites folder.

4. In the left tree pane, click the **MyBranchXX** (where *XX* is the number of your server) site to show a list of objects it contains in the right details pane.

5. In the right pane, double-click **NTDS Site Settings** to display the NTDS Site Settings Properties dialog box.

6. Check the box next to **Enable Universal Group Membership Caching**, as shown in Figure 6-7.

NOTE   In your lab environment, there is currently no domain controller located at the MyBranch*XX* site. To take advantage of universal group caching in a production environment, a domain controller would need to be located at the MyBranch*XX* site.

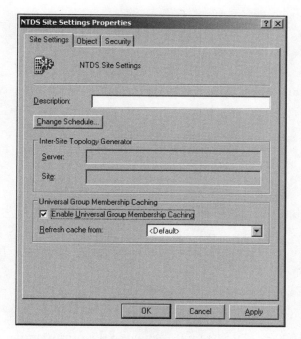

Figure 6-7   Enabling universal group caching

7. Ensure that the **Refresh cache from** drop-down list box is set to **<Default>**. With <Default> selected, domain controllers in this site will automatically locate the closest possible global catalog server from which to cache.

8. Click **OK**.

9. Close Active Directory Sites and Services.

10. Log off your server if you do not intend to continue immediately to the next project. Otherwise, stay logged on.

Certification Objectives

Objectives for Microsoft Exam #70-294: Planning, Implementing, and Maintaining a Microsoft Windows Server 2003 Active Directory Infrastructure:

■ Implement an Active Directory directory service forest and domain structure.

REVIEW QUESTIONS

1. Which of the following sites would be a good candidate for implementing universal group caching?

   a. a site with one global catalog server

   b. a site with no global catalog servers

   c. any site with more than one global catalog server

   d. any site

2. Which of the following tools do you use to implement universal group caching?

   a. Active Directory Domains and Trusts

   b. Active Directory Sites and Services

   c. Active Directory Users and Computers

   d. Active Directory Schema

3. Universal group caching is enabled from the properties of the _____ object.

4. Which of the following is a prerequisite for universal group caching to function correctly?

   a. The site must contain at least one domain controller.

   b. The site cannot contain any domain controllers.

   c. Exchange Server 2000 cannot be implemented in the organization.

   d. More than one subnet must be defined in the site.

5. When universal group membership caching is enabled, domain controllers within that site will provide the same level of functionality as a global catalog server. True or False?

LAB 6.6 IDENTIFYING REPLICATION PARTNERS

Objectives

The goal of this lab is to learn how you can use Active Directory Sites and Services to identify the replication topology of domain controllers.

Materials Required

This lab will require the following:

- A Windows Server 2003 setup, as directed at the front of this lab manual

Estimated completion time: **5 minutes**

Activity Background

Each domain controller has one or more replication partners, each identified by a connection object. Connection objects are unidirectional (one-way), not bidirectional (two-way). Connection objects identify from which other domain controllers a given domain controller will pull updates. In this activity, you will learn how to use Active Directory Sites and Services to view a domain controller's replication partners.

Activity

1. If necessary, start your server and log on using the **Administrator** account in the **CHILDXX** domain (where *XX* is the number of the forest root domain for which your server is a domain controller) using the password **Password01**.

2. Click **Start**, select **Administrative Tools**, and then click **Active Directory Sites and Services**.

3. If necessary, in the left tree pane, expand the **Sites** folder.

4. In the left tree pane, expand the **MySiteXX** (where *XX* is the number of your server) site and then expand the **Servers** folder.

5. In the left tree pane, expand **SERVERXX** (where *XX* is the number of your server), right-click **NTDS Settings**, and then click **Properties**.

6. Click the **Connections** tab, as shown in Figure 6-8 (your screen may appear slightly different depending on which projects your partner has finished). Note the domain controller(s) that your domain controller is replicating to and from.

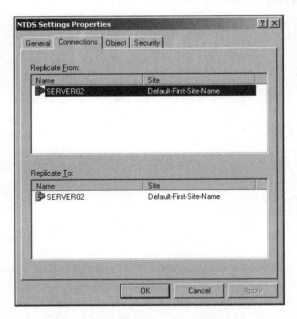

Figure 6-8 Identifying replication partners

7. Click **Cancel**.

8. In the left tree pane, click the **NTDS Settings** object to show a list of inbound connection objects that have been automatically created, as shown in Figure 6-9. The Knowledge Consistency Checker (KCC) is responsible for creating these connections between domain controllers within the same site. The KCC is a service that runs on every domain controller in a site. Similarly, the Inter-Site Topology Generator (ISTG) is responsible for creating these connections between domain controllers located in different sites. One domain controller in each site is selected as the ISTG.

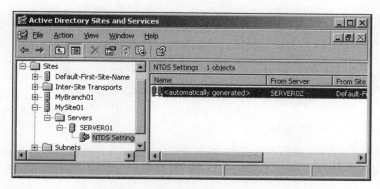

Figure 6-9   Inbound connection objects

9. Right-click the connection object that is from **SERVERXX** (where *XX* is the number of your partner's server) and then click **Replicate Now**.

10. If you receive a message box stating that the connection is between a domain controller in a different site, click **OK**. You have now manually started domain controller replication.

11. Close Active Directory Sites and Services.

12. Log off your server.

Certification Objectives

Objectives for Microsoft Exam #70-294: Planning, Implementing, and Maintaining a Microsoft Windows Server 2003 Active Directory Infrastructure:

- Monitor Active Directory replication failures.

REVIEW QUESTIONS

1. You can view the current replication partners for a domain controller by accessing the Connections tab in the properties of which object?

   a. NTDS Settings

   b. Site

   c. Subnet

   d. Domain

2. The _____ is responsible for adding replication connections for domain controllers within a site.

3. The _____ is responsible for adding replication connections for domain controllers between sites.

4. You can manually start the replication process. True or False?

5. By default, replication connections are created in which of the following ways?

   a. only manually, by the administrator

   b. automatically, by the KCC and ISTG

   c. automatically, by the RPC and SMTP transports

   d. automatically, by the global catalog

7

ACTIVE DIRECTORY REPLICATION

Labs included in this chapter:

♦ Lab 7.1 Using Event Viewer to Troubleshoot Active Directory Replication

♦ Lab 7.2 Using DNSLint to Troubleshoot Active Directory Replication

♦ Lab 7.3 Using REPADMIN to Troubleshoot Active Directory Replication

♦ Lab 7.4 Generating a Replication Report Using REPLMON

♦ Lab 7.5 Using Event Viewer to Troubleshoot SYSVOL Replication

Microsoft MCSE Exam #70-294 Objectives	
Objective	Lab
Monitor Active Directory replication failures.	7.1, 7.2, 7.3, 7.4, 7.5
Troubleshoot Active Directory.	7.1, 7.2, 7.3, 7.4, 7.5

Lab 7.1 Using Event Viewer to Troubleshoot Active Directory Replication

Objectives

The goal of this lab is to learn how to use Event Viewer to troubleshoot Active Directory replication.

Materials Required

This lab will require the following:

- A Windows Server 2003 setup, as directed at the front of this lab manual

Estimated completion time: **5 minutes**

Activity Background

Many times certain problems with Active Directory will go unnoticed or will be masked by other problems. One resource for administrators to troubleshoot Active Directory issues, or to simply check if everything is running smoothly, is the Directory Service event log, which contains informational notices, warnings, and errors regarding Active Directory. In this activity, you will use Event Viewer to view the Directory Service event log.

ACTIVITY

Activity

1. If necessary, start your server and log on using the **Administrator** account in the **CHILDXX** domain (where *XX* is the number of the forest root domain for which your server is a domain controller) using the password **Password01**.

2. Click **Start**, select **Administrative Tools**, and then click **Event Viewer**.

3. In the left tree pane, click **Directory Service** to display a list of directory service events in the right details pane, as shown in Figure 7-1. Note that if your partner's server has been offline, you may notice many warning and error messages.

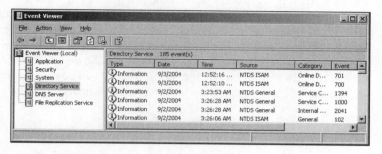

Figure 7-1   Directory Service events

4. In the right details pane, click the **Event column header** (that is, the word "Event") to sort the events by Event ID. Locate an event with the number 701 and then double-click the event (if multiple events with ID 701 are listed, choose one). The event's details are displayed, as shown in Figure 7-2.

NOTE   If you can't find an event with the ID 701, select another event.

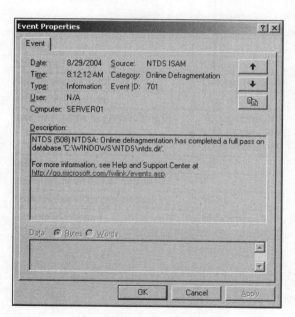

Figure 7-2   Event details

5. Click **OK**.

6. To filter the list of events, right-click **Directory Service** in the left tree pane and then click **Properties**.

NOTE Note the action that will occur when the log file reaches its maximum size. By default, old events are overwritten when the log becomes full. You can configure the log to overwrite old events only if they are a certain number of days old. You can also configure the log never to overwrite old events, but you will periodically need to clear the log manually by right-clicking the log and selecting Clear All Events. This action will free up log space. If you do not clear the log and it becomes full, new Directory Service events will not be logged.

7. Click the **Filter** tab.

8. In the **Event ID** text box, enter **701** (or the ID of the alternative event you selected in Step 4), as shown in Figure 7-3.

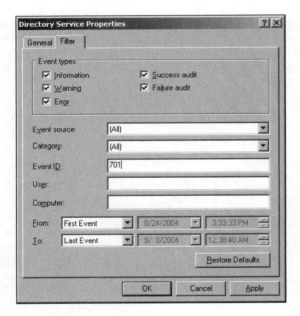

Figure 7-3   Setting up filtering

9. Click **OK**. The list of events is filtered to show only events with the Event ID you entered.

10. Close Event Viewer.

11. Log off your server if you do not intend to continue immediately to the next project. Otherwise, stay logged on.

Certification Objectives

Objectives for Microsoft Exam #70-294: Planning, Implementing, and Maintaining a Microsoft Windows Server 2003 Active Directory Infrastructure:

- Monitor Active Directory replication failures.

- Troubleshoot Active Directory.

REVIEW QUESTIONS

1. The _____ log is the primary log file in Event Viewer used to troubleshoot Active Directory-related events.

2. Windows Server 2003 will overwrite events by default when a log in Event Viewer becomes full. True or False?

3. Which of the following are ways that you can access Event Viewer on a Windows Server 2003 system? (Choose all that apply.)

   a. via the Administrative Tools menu

   b. by adding the Event Viewer snap-in to a custom MMC

   c. via the Computer Management MMC console

   d. via the Services MMC console

4. You walk into the server room one morning and notice a message at the Windows Server 2003 console that the Directory Service log is full. Which of the following might be true?

   a. The Directory Service log is not enabled.

   b. The Directory Service log is set to Do not overwrite events.

   c. The Directory Service log is set to Do not clear log.

   d. The Event Log service has been disabled.

5. The Directory Service log contains hundreds of entries, but you only want to look at error events associated with the KCC. How can you do this?

   a. Create a trap.

   b. Turn off recording of the information and warning events.

   c. Set up a filter.

   d. Print out the log so that it is easier to read.

7

LAB 7.2 USING DNSLINT TO TROUBLESHOOT ACTIVE DIRECTORY REPLICATION

Objectives

The goal of this lab is to learn how to use DNSLint to troubleshoot Active Directory replication issues related to DNS configuration.

Materials Required

This lab will require the following:

- A Windows Server 2003 setup, as directed at the front of this lab manual

Estimated completion time: **10 minutes**

Activity Background

DNSLint is included with the Windows Server 2003 support tools and is designed to check if a domain controller's records are correctly registered in DNS. If the support tools have not yet been installed, you can install them by running SUPTOOLS.MSI from the Windows Server 2003 CD. The file is located in *X*:\SUPPORT\TOOLS, where *X* is the letter of your CD-ROM drive.

ACTIVITY

Activity

1. If necessary, start your server and log on using the **Administrator** account in the **CHILDXX** domain (where *XX* is the number of the forest root domain for which your server is a domain controller) using the password **Password01**.

2. Click **Start** and then click **Command Prompt**.

3. Type **DNSLint /ad 192.168.1.XX /s 192.168.1.XX** (where *XX* is the number of your server, without any leading zeros), as shown in Figure 7-4, and then press **Enter**.

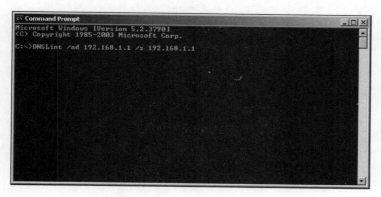

Figure 7-4   Using DNSLint

NOTE

The */ad* parameter specifies a domain controller that contains the GUIDs of all domain controllers in the forest. (Every single domain controller in the forest should have a list of every other domain controller's GUIDs in its configuration naming context.) The */s* parameter specifies a DNS server that is authoritative for the *_msdcs.forest root domain* (in this example _msdcs.child*XX*.supercorp.net) zone. DNSLint uses the GUIDs from the Active Directory configuration partition and confirms that the corresponding CNAME and A records are contained on all authoritative DNS name servers for the zone.

7

4. After DNSLint finishes, an Internet Explorer window opens containing the report, as shown in Figure 7-5. Note where the report has been saved automatically by looking in the Address bar of Internet Explorer. Note the domain controllers for which GUIDs were found, which DNS servers were checked, and if there were any warnings or errors (which appear in yellow and red, respectively).

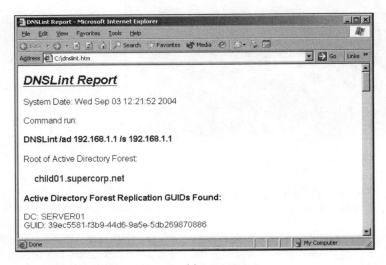

Figure 7-5   Report generated by DNSLint

5. Close Internet Explorer.

6. After answering the review questions, close the **Command Prompt** window.

7. Log off your server if you do not intend to continue immediately to the next project. Otherwise, stay logged on.

Certification Objectives

Objectives for Microsoft Exam #70-294: Planning, Implementing, and Maintaining a Microsoft Windows Server 2003 Active Directory Infrastructure:

- Monitor Active Directory replication failures.

- Troubleshoot Active Directory.

REVIEW QUESTIONS

1. You can use the _____ parameter of the DNSLint command to generate a text report, in addition to the html report.

2. You can use the _____ parameter of the DNSLint command to specify the name of the report file that is created.

3. You can use the _____ parameter of the DNSLint command to specify that if a file already exists with the same name, it should be overwritten without prompting.

4. If DNSLint reports that no DNS server has records for a given domain controller, how can you reregister the domain controller-related records in DNS?

   a. Restart the Net Logon service.

   b. Run ipconfig /registerdns.

   c. Run ipconfig /flushdns.

   d. Run nbtstat -RR.

5. If DNSLint reports that it is unable to contact a DNS server that you know has been decommissioned, how can you resolve the issue?

   a. Remove the decommissioned server's Start of Authority (SOA) record from the DNS zone.

   b. Remove the old name server's Name Server (NS) record from the DNS zone.

   c. Remove the old name server's Primary Server (PS) record from the DNS zone.

   d. Reconfigure the server's TCP/IP settings to use another DNS server.

7

LAB 7.3 USING REPADMIN TO TROUBLESHOOT ACTIVE DIRECTORY REPLICATION

Objectives

The goal of this lab is to learn how to use REPADMIN to troubleshoot Active Directory replication.

Materials Required

This lab will require the following:

- A Windows Server 2003 setup, as directed at the front of this lab manual

Estimated completion time: **10 minutes**

Activity Background

REPADMIN is another tool included with the Windows Server 2003 support tools that can be used to troubleshoot replication. REPADMIN can be used to view if a particular change has replicated to a given domain controller, view up-to-dateness vector data, and more. In this activity, you will use REPADMIN to determine which domain controller was the last to update a particular attribute.

Activity

1. If necessary, start your server and log on using the **Administrator** account in the **CHILDXX** domain (where *XX* is the number of the forest root domain for which your server is a domain controller) using the password **Password01**.

2. Click **Start** and then click **Command Prompt**.

3. Type **REPADMIN /showmeta "CN=Administrator,CN=Users, DC=childZZ,DC=supercorp,DC=net" SERVERXX.childZZ. supercorp.net** (where *ZZ* is the number of the domain for which your server is a domain controller and *XX* is the number of your server) and then press **Enter**. A list of attributes of the object is displayed, as shown in Figure 7-6 (you may need to scroll up).

The last two columns of REPADMIN's output (Ver and Attribute) may wrap to the next line. To send the output of the REPADMIN command to a file rather than to the screen, you can add **>> C:\file.txt** at the end of the above command (where C:\file.txt is the file you would like the output of REPADMIN to be directed). You can then open the file in a text editor such as Notepad to view the columns without having them wrap to the next line.

Figure 7-6   Output of REPADMIN command

4. Click **Start** and then click **Command Prompt** to open an additional Command Prompt.

5. Type **REPADMIN /showmeta "CN=Administrator,CN=Users, DC=childZZ,DC=supercorp,DC=net" SERVER***YY***.child***ZZ***. supercorp.net** (where *ZZ* is the number of the domain for which your server is a domain controller and *YY* is the number of your *partner's* server) and then press **Enter**.

6. Locate the lastLogonTimestamp attribute in both Command Prompt windows. Compare the attribute from both servers to determine whether changes have replicated from one server to the other. If changes have replicated, determine if your server or your partner's server was the last domain controller to perform a write operation on the attribute.

7. After answering the review questions, close both Command Prompt windows.

8. Log off your server if you do not intend to continue immediately to the next project. Otherwise, stay logged on.

Certification Objectives

Objectives for Microsoft Exam #70-294: Planning, Implementing, and Maintaining a Microsoft Windows Server 2003 Active Directory Infrastructure:

- Monitor Active Directory replication failures.

- Troubleshoot Active Directory.

7

REVIEW QUESTIONS

1. In order to use the REPADMIN tool, the Windows Server 2003 _____ must be installed.

2. When specifying a server name with the REPADMIN /showmeta command, which format must you use?

   a. Relative Distinguished Name

   b. Distinguished Name

   c. Fully Qualified Domain Name

   d. GUID Name

3. Which of the following can you compare between servers to determine whether a specific change has replicated from one server to another when using the REPADMIN command?

   a. version number

   b. originating timestamp

   c. originating USN and originating timestamp

   d. originating DC and originating USN

4. You can only compare two USNs when they are from which of the following domain controllers?

   a. both from direct replication partners

   b. both from the same domain controller

   c. both from domain controllers in the same domain

   d. both from domain controllers in the same forest

5. If the same attribute on an object is updated on two different domain controllers at the same time, which of the following are used to resolve the conflict? (Choose all that apply, placing in order from first to last.)

   a. originating timestamp

   b. originating USN

   c. originating database GUID

   d. version number

LAB 7.4 GENERATING A REPLICATION REPORT USING REPLMON

Objectives

The goal of this lab is to learn how to create a replication report using REPLMON. REPLMON is included with the Windows Server 2003 support tools.

Materials Required

This lab will require the following:

- A Windows Server 2003 setup, as directed at the front of this lab manual

Estimated completion time: **10 minutes**

Activity Background

REPLMON (or Replication Monitor) is yet another tool included with the Windows Server 2003 support tools that can be used to troubleshoot replication. In this activity, you will learn how REPLMON can be used to generate a replication report, which contains a lot of useful information for troubleshooting.

Activity

1. If necessary, start your server and log on using the **Administrator** account in the **CHILDXX** domain (where *XX* is the number of the forest root domain for which your server is a domain controller) using the password **Password01**.

2. Click **Start** and then click **Run**.

3. Type **REPLMON** in the drop-down box and click **OK**.

4. In the left pane, right-click **Monitored Servers** and then click **Add Monitored Server**.

5. Ensure that the Add the server explicitly by name button is selected and then click **Next**.

6. In the Enter the name of the server to monitor explicitly textbox, enter **SERVERXX** (where *XX* is the number of your server).

7. Click **Finish**.

8. In the left tree pane, right-click **SERVERXX** (where *XX* is the number of your server) and then click **Generate Status Report**.

9. In the Save As dialog box, navigate to the My Documents folder. Name the file **SERVERXX-ReplReport** (where *XX* is the number of your server) and then click **Save**.

10. The Report Options window will appear. Configure the options as shown in Figure 7-7.

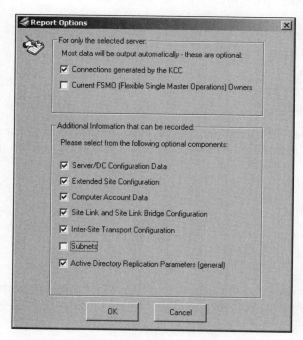

Figure 7-7   Report Options window

11. Click **OK**.

12. Once the report has generated, click **OK** on the Report Status window.

13. Close Active Directory Replication Monitor.

14. Click **Start** and then click **Windows Explorer**. The folder selected should automatically be your My Documents folder. If not, navigate to your My Documents folder in the left tree pane.

15. In the right pane, double-click **SERVERXX-ReplReport.log** (where *XX* is the number of your server). Scroll through and review the report.

16. For the domain directory partition, note the USN (Update Sequence Number) of the last property updated from your partner's server.

17. For the domain directory partition, note when replication was last attempted with your partner's server, and when replication was last successful.

18. Close the report file.

19. Close Windows Explorer.

20. Log off your server.

Certification Objectives

Objectives for Microsoft Exam #70-294: Planning, Implementing, and Maintaining a Microsoft Windows Server 2003 Active Directory Infrastructure:

- Monitor Active Directory replication failures.

- Troubleshoot Active Directory.

REVIEW QUESTIONS

1. Which of the following is used to identify replication partners, for example in DNS, and will not change if the Active Directory Database is restored from backup?

   a. Server GUID

   b. Replication GUID

   c. Database GUID

   d. KCC GUID

2. Which of the following is used to identify replication partners, for example in a High-Watermark table, and can change if the Active Directory Database is restored from backup?

   a. Server GUID

   b. Replication GUID

   c. Database GUID

   d. KCC GUID

3. USN stands for _____.

4. The primary tool used to view the replication topology in a Windows Server 2003 Active Directory environment graphically is _____.

5. How often does replication occur between domain controllers in different sites in an Active Directory environment by default?

   a. every 15 minutes

   b. every hour

   c. every 3 hours

   d. every 24 hours

LAB 7.5 USING EVENT VIEWER TO TROUBLESHOOT SYSVOL REPLICATION

7

Objectives

The goal of this lab is to learn how to use Event Viewer to troubleshoot SYSVOL replication.

Materials Required

This lab will require the following:

- A Windows Server 2003 setup, as directed at the front of this lab manual

Estimated completion time: **10 minutes**

Activity Background

Whereas the Directory Service event log holds events related to Active Directory, the File Replication Service event log holds events related to FRS. (Recall that FRS is used to replicate SYSVOL.) If network scripts or group policy objects don't seem to be updating on all domain controllers, check that FRS replication is working correctly. In this activity, you will use Event Viewer to view the File Replication Service event log.

ACTIVITY

Activity

1. If necessary, start your server and log on using the **Administrator** account in the **CHILDXX** domain (where *XX* is the number of the forest root domain for which your server is a domain controller) using the password **Password01**.

2. Click **Start**, select **Administrative Tools**, and then click **Event Viewer**.

3. In the left tree pane, click **File Replication Service** to display a list of FRS events in the right details pane, as shown in Figure 7-8. Note that if your partner's server has been offline, you may notice many warnings and error messages.

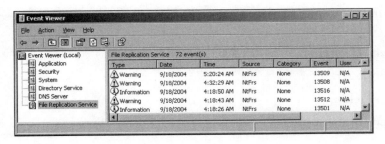

Figure 7-8   File Replication Service events

4. Double-click an event entry with the ID 13501. Use the skills you learned in Activity 7-1 to locate an event with this ID, if necessary.

TIP

Event ID 13501 indicates when FRS is in the process of starting. If an error occurs and FRS is unable to start, an error entry indicating the problem will typically follow event ID 13501. Additionally, event ID 13502 indicates when the FRS service is in the process of stopping. Event ID 13503 indicates when the FRS service has stopped.

NOTE

It is not necessary to memorize the meanings of the different event IDs. Event Viewer, Help and Support, and *support.microsoft.com* can all be used to locate information on the meaning of various event IDs.

5. Close the Event Properties window.

6. Double-click an event entry with the ID 13566, as shown in Figure 7-9. Use the skills you learned in Activity 7-1 to locate an event with this ID, if necessary.

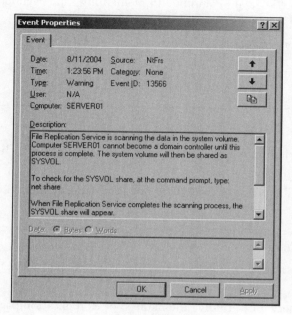

Figure 7-9   Event ID 13566 details

Before a server can act as a domain controller, FRS must first scan the files in the SYSVOL share. Event ID 13566 indicates that this process is occurring. When the process has completed, event ID 13516 will be logged and FRS will no longer prevent the server from acting as a domain controller.

7. Close the Event Properties window.

8. Double-click an event entry with the ID 13508. Use the skills you learned in Activity 7-1 to locate an event with this ID, if necessary.

Event ID 13508 indicates that FRS is having trouble replicating a share from another server. The servers and the share that FRS is unable to replicate are listed in the event's properties. When replication of the share starts to occur correctly again, event ID 13509 will be logged.

9. Close the Event Properties window.

10. Close Event Viewer.

11. Log off your server.

Certification Objectives

Objectives for Microsoft Exam #70-294: Planning, Implementing, and Maintaining a Microsoft Windows Server 2003 Active Directory Infrastructure:

- Monitor Active Directory replication failures.

- Troubleshoot Active Directory.

REVIEW QUESTIONS

1. The first step in troubleshooting replication of SYSVOL is to do which of the following?

   a. Confirm that the files being replicated are not automatically filtered out by FRS.

   b. If they exist, resolve any issues with Active Directory replication before troubleshooting SYSVOL replication.

   c. Confirm that there is sufficient disk space available where the SYSVOL folder is stored.

   d. Confirm that the server can resolve the name(s) of its replication partner(s).

2. By default, FRS does not replicate files that end in which of the following extensions? (Choose all that apply.)

   a. .bak

   b. .vbs

   c. .tmp

   d. .bat

3. After you restart a domain controller, you notice that it is not working correctly. You notice that the last entry in the File Replication Service log indicates that FRS is starting. Which of the following consoles could you use to confirm that FRS has started, or is still in the process of starting?

   a. Services console

   b. Distributed File System console

   c. Active Directory Users and Computers console

   d. Active Directory Sites and Services console

4. For FRS to work correctly, a server must be able to resolve which type of name?

   a. its replication partner's NetBIOS name

   b. its replication partner's hostname

   c. its replication partner's FQDN

   d. its replication partner's distinguished name

5. The topology used to replicate the SYSVOL share uses which of the following?

   a. a full mesh topology

   b. a partial mesh topology from the PDC emulator

   c. a star topology from the PDC emulator

   d. the same topology that the KCC generates to replicate the domain partition

8

ACTIVE DIRECTORY OPERATIONS MASTERS

Labs included in this chapter:

♦ Lab 8.1 Identifying the Domain-Wide FSMO Role Holders for Another Domain

♦ Lab 8.2 Using REPLMON to Identify and Test Operations Masters

♦ Lab 8.3 Using NETDOM to Identify Operations Masters

♦ Lab 8.4 Using NTDSUTIL to Identify Operations Masters

Microsoft MCSE Exam #70-294 Objectives	
Objective	Lab
Plan flexible operations master role placement.	8.1, 8.2, 8.3,8.4
Troubleshoot Active Directory.	8.1, 8.2, 8.3, 8.4

Lab 8.1 Identifying the Domain-Wide FSMO Role Holders for Another Domain

Objectives

The goal of this lab is to learn how to use Active Directory Users and Computers to identify operations masters in another domain.

Materials Required

This lab will require the following:

- A Windows Server 2003 setup, as directed at the front of this lab manual

Estimated completion time: **5 minutes**

Activity Background

In addition to managing objects and domain-wide FSMO role holders for the local domain, you can also use Active Directory Users and Computers to manage objects and domain-wide FSMO role holders for another domain (assuming you have the necessary permissions). In this lab, you will learn how to target the Active Directory Users and Computers console to another trusting domain.

Activity

1. If necessary, start your server and log on using the **Administrator** account in the **CHILDXX** domain (where *XX* is the number of the forest root domain for which your server is a domain controller) using the password **Password01**.

2. Click **Start**, select **Administrative Tools**, and then click **Active Directory Users and Computers**.

3. In the left tree pane, right-click the **Active Directory Users and Computers** node and then click **Connect to Domain**.

4. In the Domain text box, enter **supercorp.net** as shown in Figure 8-1.

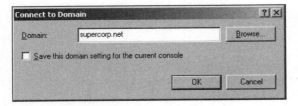

Figure 8-1   Specifying domain to establish connection

5. Click **OK**. The Active Directory Users and Computers console will connect to a domain controller in the supercorp.net domain. Note that supercorp.net is a domain in another forest that you have already established a trust relationship with. (You can use Steps 3–5 to connect to a domain in the same forest as well.)

6. In the left tree pane, right-click **supercorp.net** and then click **Operations Masters**. The domain-wide FSMO role holders are displayed for the super-corp.net domain on their respective tabs, as shown in Figure 8-2.

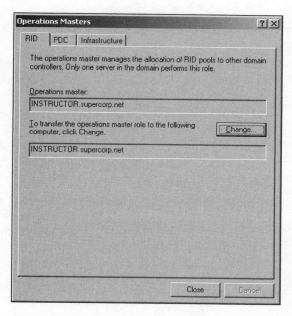

Figure 8-2   Domain-wide operations masters for remote domain

7. Click **Close**.

8. Close Active Directory Users and Computers.

9. Log off your server if you do not intend to continue immediately to the next project. Otherwise, stay logged on.

Certification Objectives

Objectives for Microsoft Exam #70-294: Planning, Implementing, and Maintaining a Microsoft Windows Server 2003 Active Directory Infrastructure:

- Plan flexible operations master role placement.

- Troubleshoot Active Directory.

REVIEW QUESTIONS

1. Which of the following tools can you use to identify the server that holds the PDC emulator FSMO role for another domain?

   a. Active Directory Users and Computers

   b. Active Directory Domains and Trusts

   c. Active Directory Sites and Services

   d. Active Directory Schema

2. Which of the following are domain-wide FSMO roles? (Choose all that apply.)

   a. Infrastructure Master

   b. Domain Master

   c. PDC emulator

   d. RID Master

   e. SID Master

3. By default, you must be a member of which of the following groups in order to move the PDC Emulator role between domain controllers?

   a. Schema Admins

   b. Enterprise Admins

   c. Domain Admins

   d. FSMO Admins

4. Which of the following physical locations would be the best place to locate the RID Master?

   a. in a central point on the network

   b. in the same site as the schema master

   c. in the site where most new security principles are created

   d. Physical placement of the PDC emulator is not a concern.

5. How many domain controllers can hold the schema master role in a forest with three domains?

   a. 0

   b. 1

   c. 2

   d. 3

Lab 8.2 Using REPLMON to Identify and Test Operations Masters

Objectives

The goal of this lab is to learn how to use REPLMON to identify operations masters and verify connectivity.

Materials Required

This lab will require the following:

- A Windows Server 2003 setup, as directed at the front of this lab manual

Estimated completion time: **5 minutes**

Activity Background

8

The Active Directory Replication Monitor (REPLMON) is a powerful graphical tool that you can use to monitor and troubleshoot Active Directory Replication. In this lab, you will learn how to use REPLMON to view operations masters. Keep in mind that REPLMON will display the FSMO role holders that are listed in the directory database of the domain controller you select. When a role is moved or seized, some domain controllers may not be aware of the change until the change has replicated to the domain controllers.

Activity

1. If necessary, start your server and log on using the **Administrator** account in the **CHILDXX** domain (where *XX* is the number of the forest root domain for which your server is a domain controller) using the password **Password01**.

2. Click **Start** and then click **Run**.

3. Type **REPLMON** in the drop-down box and click **OK**.

4. In the left pane, right-click **Monitored Servers** and then click **Add Monitored Server**.

5. Ensure that the Add the server explicitly by name radio button is selected and then click **Next**.

6. In the Enter the name of the server to monitor explicitly text box, enter **SERVERXX** (where *XX* is the number of your server).

7. Click **Finish**.

8. In the left tree pane, right-click **SERVERXX** (where *XX* is the number of your server) and then click **Properties**.

9. Click the **FSMO Roles** tab. The list of role holders according to your domain controller is displayed, as shown in Figure 8-3.

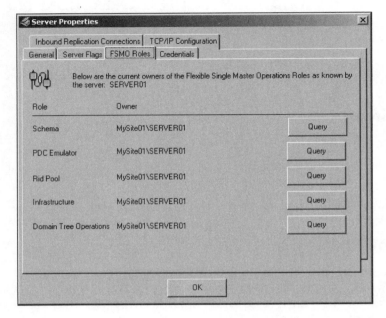

Figure 8-3   Operations masters listed using Replication Monitor

10. Click the **Query** button for the PDC Emulator role. This will test communications between your server and the PDC emulator.

11. A message box will appear stating whether communication was successful, as shown in Figure 8-4. Click **OK**.

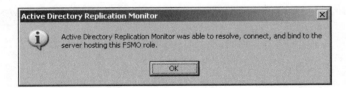

Figure 8-4   Operations master communication test results

12. Click **OK** to close the Server Properties window.

13. Close Replication Monitor.

14. Log off your server if you do not intend to continue immediately to the next project. Otherwise, stay logged on.

Certification Objectives

Objectives for Microsoft Exam #70-294: Planning, Implementing, and Maintaining a Microsoft Windows Server 2003 Active Directory Infrastructure:

- Plan flexible operations master role placement.

- Troubleshoot Active Directory.

REVIEW QUESTIONS

1. If communication with the PDC Emulator fails, which of the following could occur?

   a. You may not be able to add new users.

   b. You may not be able to add new domains.

   c. Password updates may take longer to propagate.

   d. References to objects in other domains may not update.

2. If communication with the Infrastructure Master fails, which of the following could occur?

   a. You may not be able to add new users.

   b. You may not be able to add new domains.

   c. Password updates may take longer to propagate.

   d. References to objects in other domains may not update.

3. If communication with the RID Master fails, which of the following could occur?

   a. You may not be able to add new users.

   b. You may not be able to add new domains.

   c. Password updates may take longer to propagate.

   d. References to objects in other domains may not update.

4. You will not be able to add new class definitions to Active Directory if communication fails with which of the following operations masters?

   a. PDC Emulator

   b. RID Master

   c. Domain Naming Master

   d. Infrastructure Master

   e. Schema Master

5. You will not be able to add new domains to the forest if communication fails with which of the following operations masters?

   a. PDC Emulator

   b. RID Master

   c. Domain Naming Master

   d. Infrastructure Master

   e. Schema Master

Lab 8.3 Using NETDOM to Identify Operations Masters

Objectives

The goal of this lab is to learn how to use NETDOM to identify operations masters for the same or a different domain.

Materials Required

This lab will require the following:

- A Windows Server 2003 setup, as directed at the front of this lab manual

Estimated completion time: **5 minutes**

Activity Background

In addition to the graphical tools you have used to view operations masters, you can also use the NETDOM command-line utility to view operations masters. In this lab, you will learn how to use NETDOM to view operations masters.

ACTIVITY

Activity

1. If necessary, start your server and log on using the **Administrator** account in the **CHILDXX** domain (where XX is the number of the forest root domain for which your server is a domain controller) using the password **Password01**.

2. Click **Start** and then click **Command Prompt**.

3. At the prompt, type **NETDOM query fsmo** and then press **Enter**. The master role holders are displayed, as shown in Figure 8-5.

Figure 8-5 Operations masters listed using NETDOM

4. Type **NETDOM query /domain:supercorp.net fsmo** and then press **Enter**. The master role holders for the supercorp.net domain are displayed. Note that the forest-wide roles for the forest in which the supercorp.net domain is located are also shown.

5. Type **exit** and then press **Enter**.

6. Log off your server if you do not intend to continue immediately to the next project. Otherwise, stay logged on.

Certification Objectives

Objectives for Microsoft Exam #70-294: Planning, Implementing, and Maintaining a Microsoft Windows Server 2003 Active Directory Infrastructure:

- Plan flexible operations master role placement.

- Troubleshoot Active Directory.

REVIEW QUESTIONS

1. You can use the _____ parameter of the NETDOM query command to specify that the query be performed on another domain.

2. You can use the NETDOM command to view both _____-wide and _____-wide FSMO roles.

3. Which of the following domain controllers should the Infrastructure Master never be placed on in a multi-domain forest?

a. a domain controller that is a PDC Emulator

b. a domain controller that is a RID Master

c. a domain controller that is a Domain Naming Master

d. a domain controller that is a Global Catalog

e. a domain controller that is a Schema Master

4. On which domain controller are all FSMO roles placed by default in the root domain? (Give a short, one-sentence answer.)

5. You can never move the schema master role to another domain controller. True or False?

LAB 8.4 USING NTDSUTIL TO IDENTIFY OPERATIONS MASTERS

Objectives

The goal of this lab is to learn how to use NTDSUTIL to identify operations masters.

Materials Required

This lab will require the following:

- A Windows Server 2003 setup, as directed at the front of this lab manual

Estimated completion time: **5 minutes**

Activity Background

In addition to the NETDOM utility, NTDSUTIL is another command-line utility that you can use to view operations masters. In this lab, you will learn how to use NTDSUTIL to view operations masters.

ACTIVITY

Activity

1. If necessary, start your server and log on using the **Administrator** account in the **CHILDXX** domain (where *XX* is the number of the forest root domain for which your server is a domain controller) using the password **Password01**.

2. Click **Start** and then click **Command Prompt**.

3. Type **NTDSUTIL** and then press **Enter**.

4. Type **domain management** and then press **Enter**.

5. Type **connections** and then press **Enter**.

6. Type **connect to server SERVERXX.childZZ.supercorp.net** (where *XX* is the number of your server and *ZZ* is the number of the forest root domain) and then press **Enter**.

7. Type **quit** and then press **Enter**.

8. Type **select operation target** and then press **Enter**.

9. Type **list roles for connected server** and then press **Enter**. The distinguished name of the server's NTDS Settings object (that holds the role) is displayed for each of the roles, as shown in Figure 8–6.

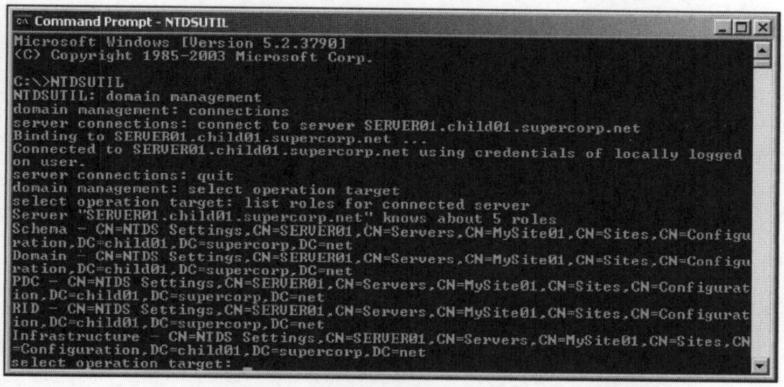

```
Command Prompt - NTDSUTIL
Microsoft Windows [Version 5.2.3790]
(C) Copyright 1985-2003 Microsoft Corp.

C:\>NTDSUTIL
NTDSUTIL: domain management
domain management: connections
server connections: connect to server SERVER01.child01.supercorp.net
Binding to SERVER01.child01.supercorp.net ...
Connected to SERVER01.child01.supercorp.net using credentials of locally logged
on user.
server connections: quit
domain management: select operation target
select operation target: list roles for connected server
Server "SERVER01.child01.supercorp.net" knows about 5 roles
Schema - CN=NTDS Settings,CN=SERVER01,CN=Servers,CN=MySite01,CN=Sites,CN=Configu
ration,DC=child01,DC=supercorp,DC=net
Domain - CN=NTDS Settings,CN=SERVER01,CN=Servers,CN=MySite01,CN=Sites,CN=Configu
ration,DC=child01,DC=supercorp,DC=net
PDC - CN=NTDS Settings,CN=SERVER01,CN=Servers,CN=MySite01,CN=Sites,CN=Configurat
ion,DC=child01,DC=supercorp,DC=net
RID - CN=NTDS Settings,CN=SERVER01,CN=Servers,CN=MySite01,CN=Sites,CN=Configurat
ion,DC=child01,DC=supercorp,DC=net
Infrastructure - CN=NTDS Settings,CN=SERVER01,CN=Servers,CN=MySite01,CN=Sites,CN
=Configuration,DC=child01,DC=supercorp,DC=net
select operation target:
```

Figure 8-6 Operations masters listed using NTDSUTIL

10. Type **quit** and then press **Enter**.

11. Type **quit** and then press **Enter**.

12. Type **quit** and then press **Enter**.

13. Type **exit** and then press **Enter**.

14. Log off your server.

Certification Objectives

Objectives for Microsoft Exam #70-294: Planning, Implementing, and Maintaining a Microsoft Windows Server 2003 Active Directory Infrastructure:

■ Plan flexible operations master role placement.

■ Troubleshoot Active Directory.

REVIEW QUESTIONS

1. When using NTDSUTIL to display operations masters, the distinguished name of which of the following is displayed?

   a. the domain's NTDS Settings object

   b. the server's NTDS Settings object

   c. the forest's NTDS Settings object

   d. the configuration partition's NTDS Settings object

2. To view the FSMO role holders using NTDSUTIL, issue the _____ command.

3. When connecting to a server using the NTDSUTIL connect to server command, what type of name should you provide?

   a. common name

   b. distinguished name

   c. relative distinguished name

   d. fully qualified domain name

4. You can use the NTDSUTIL command to change FSMO role holders. True or False?

5. Which of the following types of names is displayed by the NTDSUTIL command when viewing operations masters?

   a. common name

   b. distinguished name

   c. relative distinguished name

   d. fully qualified domain name

9

ACTIVE DIRECTORY AUTHENTICATION AND SECURITY

Labs included in this chapter:

- ♦ Lab 9.1 Configuring Permissions on a Folder
- ♦ Lab 9.2 Configuring Auditing on a Folder
- ♦ Lab 9.3 Working with the Security Log
- ♦ Lab 9.4 Configuring Permissions on a Registry Key

While all the labs in this chapter pertain to Active Directory, they do not map directly to any MCSE Certification Objectives.

Lab 9.1 Configuring Permissions on a Folder

Objectives

The goal of this lab is to learn how to configure NTFS permissions on a folder.

Materials Required

This lab will require the following:

- A Windows Server 2003 setup, as directed at the front of this lab manual

Estimated completion time: **5 minutes**

Activity Background

In addition to Active Directory objects, files and folders on NTFS-formatted volumes also have a DACL that can be used to control access. Once a user is authenticated on the network using Active Directory, the file or folder's DACL is used to define the authorization level a user or group has on the file or folder. In this lab, you will learn how to disable permission inheritance in order to restrict access to a folder.

ACTIVITY

Activity

1. If necessary, start your server and log on using the **Administrator** account in the **CHILDXX** domain (where *XX* is the number of the forest root domain for which your server is a domain controller) using the password **Password01**.

2. Click **Start** and then click **My Computer**.

3. Double-click the **D:** drive, which should be the second hard drive in your server. (Or double-click the drive letter specified by your instructor.)

4. On the **File** menu, select **New**, and then click **Folder**.

5. Enter **IT Docs** as the name for the new folder.

6. Right-click the **IT Docs** folder and then click **Properties**.

7. Click the **Security** tab.

8. Click the **Advanced** button.

9. Uncheck the box next to **Allow inheritable permissions from the parent to propagate to this object and all child objects**, similar to Figure 9–1.

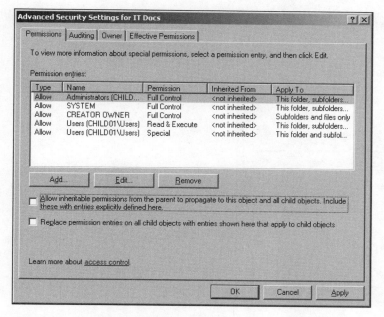

Figure 9-1   Disable inheritance of permissions from parent

10. On the Security window that appears, click **Copy**.

11. Click **OK**.

12. Remove all users and groups except Administrators and SYSTEM. You can remove a group by selecting the user or group from the Group or user names list box and then clicking **Remove**.

13. Confirm that both the Administrators and SYSTEM groups have the Full Control permission, as shown in Figure 9-2.

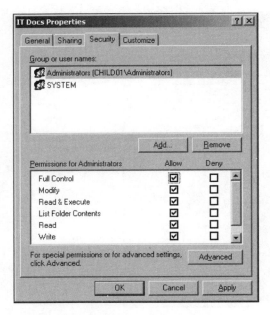

Figure 9-2 Setting permissions for a group

14. Click **OK**. The only users that can now access this folder (and files/folders in this folder) are members of the Administrators group or the operating system.

15. Close the Windows Explorer window.

16. Log off your server if you do not intend to continue immediately to the next project. Otherwise, stay logged on.

Certification Objectives

Objectives for Microsoft Exam #70-294: Planning, Implementing, and Maintaining a Microsoft Windows Server 2003 Active Directory Infrastructure:

■ Not applicable

REVIEW QUESTIONS

1. Which of the following formats provides file- and folder-level security?

   a. FAT

   b. FAT32

   c. NTFS

   d. both FAT32 and NTFS

2. NTFS permissions apply when you access a file in which of the following ways?

   a. only from the local server console

   b. only from a network path

   c. both a and b

   d. neither a nor b

3. Which of the following can you do with inheritance on files and folders?

   a. Enable inheritance, but never disable it.

   b. Disable inheritance, but never enable it.

   c. Enable and disable inheritance as needed.

   d. You can't enable or disable inheritance.

4. Unlike NTFS permissions, file share permissions apply when you access a file in which of the following ways?

   a. only from the local server console

   b. only from a network path

   c. both a and b

   d. neither a nor b

5. Which of the following stores permission entries for a folder?

   a. SACL

   b. DACL

   c. PACL

   d. AACL

9

LAB 9.2 CONFIGURING AUDITING ON A FOLDER

Objectives

The goal of this lab is to learn how to configure auditing on a folder.

Materials Required

This lab will require the following:

- A Windows Server 2003 setup, as directed at the front of this lab manual

Estimated completion time: **5 minutes**

Activity Background

In addition to Active Directory objects, files and folders on NTFS-formatted volumes also have an SACL that can be used to audit access. In this lab, you will learn how to enable auditing on a folder. Remember, in order for object access events to be logged, the Audit object access policy must be enabled.

Activity

Because you are changing a security policy that affects all domain controllers, work with your partner and perform the first part of this activity from only one of the two domain controllers of your domain.

1. If necessary, start your server and log on using the **Administrator** account in the **CHILDXX** domain (where *XX* is the number of the forest root domain for which your server is a domain controller) using the password **Password01**.

2. In order for SACLs you set on individual objects to take effect, you must ensure object access auditing is enabled. To check the status of object access auditing for only the domain controllers, start by clicking **Start**, select **Administrative Tools**, and then click **Domain Controller Security Policy**.

3. In the left tree pane, expand the **Security Settings** and **Local Policies** nodes.

4. In the left tree pane, click **Audit Policy**.

5. In the right details pane, double-click **Audit object access**.

6. Add a check next to **Success** in order to audit successful use of permissions.

7. Click **OK**.

8. Close the Domain Controllers' Security Policy window. You have now enabled object access auditing on domain controllers. (Note that the domain controllers security policy actually applies to the Domain Controllers organizational unit). Both partners may now complete the remaining steps in this activity individually.

 It may take several minutes for the domain controller's security policy to replicate to the second domain controller and then refresh. You can manually initiate **NOTE** replication using Active Directory Sites and Services if you wish.

9. Click **Start** and then click **My Computer**.

10. Double-click the **D:** drive, which should be the second hard drive in your server. (Or double-click the drive letter specified by your instructor.)

11. Right-click the **IT Docs** folder and then click **Properties**.

12. Click the **Security** tab.

13. Click the **Advanced** button.

14. Click the **Auditing** tab.

15. Click the **Add** Button.

16. Type **Administrators** and then click **OK**.

9

17. Check the **Successful** check box for the following, as shown in Figure 9-3:

- Create Files / Write Data

- Create Folders / Append Data

- Delete Subfolders and Files

- Delete

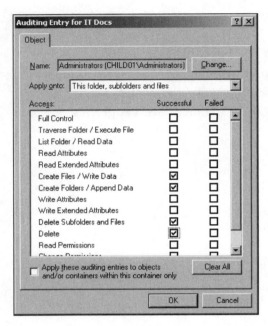

Figure 9-3   Selecting what to audit

18. Click **OK**. The auditing entry is added, as shown in Figure 9-4.

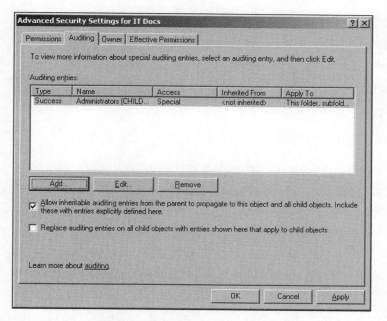

Figure 9-4   New auditing entry

19. Click **OK** to close the Advanced Security Settings window.

20. Click **OK** to close the IT Docs Properties window.

21. Close the Windows Explorer window.

22. Log off your server if you do not intend to continue immediately to the next project. Otherwise, stay logged on.

Certification Objectives

Objectives for Microsoft Exam #70-294: Planning, Implementing, and Maintaining a Microsoft Windows Server 2003 Active Directory Infrastructure:

- Not applicable

REVIEW QUESTIONS

1. Which of the following formats supports auditing?

    a. FAT

    b. FAT32

    c. NTFS

    d. both FAT32 and NTFS

2. Which of the following statements is true about auditing?

    a. The impact of auditing is negligible, so you should audit as much as possible.

    b. Excessive auditing can slow a server down, so you should use care when choosing what you audit.

    c. Auditing is not necessary if permissions have been configured correctly.

    d. Auditing is only necessary at military, government, and other high-security institutions.

3. Which of the following must you enable in the Audit Policy in order to audit events related to the file system?

    a. Object access

    b. File access

    c. Registry access

    d. Privilege use

4. Which of the following stores auditing entries on a file?

    a. SACL

    b. DACL

    c. PACL

    d. AACL

5. Which of the following does an ACE contain?

    a. the CN of a user or group

    b. the SID of a user or group

    c. the GUID of a user or group

    d. the ACL of a user or group

LAB 9.3 WORKING WITH THE SECURITY LOG

Objectives

The goal of this lab is to learn how to work with the security log.

Materials Required

This lab will require the following:

- A Windows Server 2003 setup, as directed at the front of this lab manual

Estimated completion time: **10 minutes**

Activity Background

Once auditing is configured, any auditing events are placed in the Windows Security log. An administrator can view the Security log by using Event viewer. In this lab, you will learn how to view events in the Security log as well as how to configure the log's settings.

ACTIVITY

Activity

1. If necessary, start your server and log on using the **Administrator** account in the **CHILDXX** domain (where *XX* is the number of the forest root domain for which your server is a domain controller) using the password **Password01**.

2. Click **Start** and then click **My Computer**.

3. Double-click the **D:** drive, which should be the second hard drive in your server. (Or double-click the drive letter specified by your instructor.)

4. Double-click the **IT Docs** folder.

5. On the **File** menu, select **New**, and then click **Text Document**. Accept the default file name.

6. Double-click the file you just created so that you can edit it.

7. Type **Security Audit Test** and then close the file. When prompted to save the changes, click **Yes**.

8. Right-click the file you just created and then click **Delete**. Click **Yes** when asked if you are sure you want to delete the file.

9. Close the Windows Explorer window.

10. Click **Start**, select **Administrative Tools**, and then click **Event Viewer**.

11. In the left tree pane, click **Security**.

12. In the right details pane, double-click the top entry to show its details.

9

13. Use the down arrow button to scroll through the events until you locate the first event related to the text document you were just working with. The event should look similar to Figure 9-5.

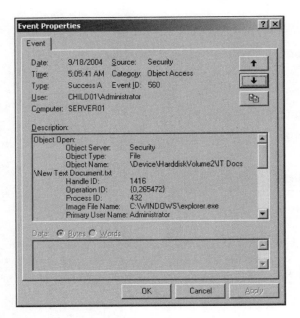

Figure 9-5   Audit event details

14. Review the details of the entry and then click **OK**.

15. In the left tree pane, right-click **Security** and then click **Properties**.

16. In the Maximum log size spin box, enter **60032**. Note that if you enter a log size that is not an increment of 64 KB, the log will be resized to the closest increment of 64 KB automatically.

17. Click the **Overwrite events older than** radio button and confirm that the number of days is set to 7, as shown in Figure 9-6. This will prevent log events from being overwritten unless they are 7 days old or more.

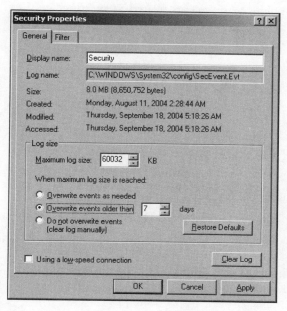

Figure 9-6   Setting Security log properties

18. Click **OK**.

19. If you are reducing the log's size, you will be prompted that the log must first be cleared before the new log size will take effect. Click **OK**.

20. In the left tree pane, right-click **Security** and then click **Clear all Events**.

21. When prompted if you want to save before clearing, click **No**. Note that an event is added that indicates who cleared the log.

22. Close Event Viewer.

23. Log off your server if you do not intend to continue immediately to the next project. Otherwise, stay logged on.

Certification Objectives

Objectives for Microsoft Exam #70-294: Planning, Implementing, and Maintaining a Microsoft Windows Server 2003 Active Directory Infrastructure:

- Not applicable

REVIEW QUESTIONS

1. Which of the following logs stores events related to auditing?

    a. Access

    b. Auditing

    c. Security

    d. System

2. When shrinking a log in Event Viewer, you must do which of the following for the change to take effect?

    a. Delete the log's .log file in the %systemroot%\logs folder.

    b. Delete the log using Event Viewer.

    c. Delete all events inside the log using the Delete key.

    d. Clear the log using Event Viewer.

3. Which of the following must you enable in the Audit Policy in order to audit events that are related to the registry?

    a. Object access

    b. File access

    c. Registry access

    d. Privilege use

4. Log file size must be set in increments of:

    a. 16 K

    b. 32 K

    c. 64 K

    d. 128 K

5. An administrator can clear the security log using Event Viewer without leaving any indication that he or she cleared the log. True or False?

LAB 9.4 CONFIGURING PERMISSIONS ON A REGISTRY KEY

Objectives

The goal of this lab is to learn how to configure permissions on a registry key.

Materials Required

This lab will require the following:

- A Windows Server 2003 setup, as directed at the front of this lab manual

Estimated completion time: 5 minutes

Activity Background

In addition to Active Directory objects, registry keys also have a DACL that can be used to control access. Once a user is authenticated on the network using Active Directory, the registry key's DACL is used to define the authorization level a user or group has on the registry key. In this lab, you will learn how to grant permissions on a registry key.

Activity

1. If necessary, start your server and log on using the **Administrator** account in the **CHILDXX** domain (where *XX* is the number of the forest root domain for which your server is a domain controller) using the password **Password01**.

2. Click **Start** and then click **Run**.

3. Type **regedit** and then click **OK**.

4. In the left tree pane, expand the following nodes, if necessary:
   - My Computer
   - HKEY_LOCAL_MACHINE
   - SOFTWARE

5. Right-click the **ODBC** key in the left tree pane and then click **Permissions**.

You can only set permissions on keys, not individual values.

6. Click the **Advanced** button.

7. In the Permission entries list box, select **Authenticated Users** and then click **Edit**.

9

8. Check the **Allow** check box for the following, as shown in Figure 9-7:

- Set Value
- Create Subkey
- Create Link
- Delete

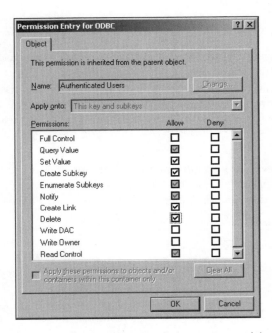

Figure 9-7   Setting permissions on a registry key

9. Click **OK**.

10. Click **OK** to close the Advanced Security Settings window.

11. Click **OK** to close the ODBC key permissions window.

12. Close Registry Editor.

13. Log off your server.

Certification Objectives

Objectives for Microsoft Exam #70-294: Planning, Implementing, and Maintaining a Microsoft Windows Server 2003 Active Directory Infrastructure:

- Not applicable

REVIEW QUESTIONS

1. Permissions can be set on which of the following?

   a. keys

   b. values

   c. both keys and values

   d. neither keys nor values

2. In Windows Server 2003, what is the difference between regedit and regedt32?

   a. Nothing, they are the same program.

   b. Regedt32 can configure permissions and regedit cannot.

   c. Regedit can configure permissions and regedt32 cannot.

   d. Regedit is a command–line tool whereas regedt32 has a graphical user interface.

3. The only permissions that can be set on a registry key are Full Control and Read. True or False?

4. Like every file on a NTFS drive, every key in the registry has which of the following associated with it?

   a. an Administrator

   b. an Owner

   c. a Master

   d. a Delegate

5. When determining a user's level of access to a registry key, the Windows security subsystem compares SIDs contained in the user's _____ to ACEs stored in the key's DACL.

9

10

MANAGING USERS, GROUPS, COMPUTERS, AND RESOURCES

Labs included in this chapter:

◆ Lab 10.1 Creating a User Account Template

◆ Lab 10.2 Exporting Active Directory User Accounts Using CSVDE

◆ Lab 10.3 Importing Active Directory User Accounts Using CSVDE

◆ Lab 10.4 Creating Groups Using DSADD

◆ Lab 10.5 Modifying Groups Using DSMOD

Microsoft MCSE Exam #70-294 Objectives	
Objective	Lab
Manage an Active Directory forest and domain structure.	10.1, 10.2, 10.3, 10.4, 10.5

Lab 10.1 Creating a User Account Template

Objectives

The goal of this lab is to learn how to create a user account for use as a template for other user accounts.

Materials Required

This lab will require the following:

- A Windows Server 2003 setup, as directed at the front of this lab manual

Estimated completion time: **10 minutes**

Activity Background

Many users in an organization share common account properties. Rather than having to set the common properties over and over for every new user account, an administrator can create a user account template and then copy the template to create new user accounts. In this lab, you will learn how to create a template account and then create a new user based on the template.

Activity

1. If necessary, start your server and log on using the **Administrator** account in the **CHILDXX** domain (where *XX* is the number of the forest root domain for which your server is a domain controller) using the password **Password01**.

2. Click **Start**, select **Administrative Tools**, and then click **Active Directory Users and Computers**.

3. If necessary, in the left tree pane, expand the **childXX.supercorp.net** node (where *XX* is the number of the forest root domain for which your server is a domain controller).

4. In the left tree pane, expand the **North America XX** organizational unit (where *XX* is the number of your server).

5. In the left tree pane, click the **Atlanta** organizational unit, under your North America *XX* organizational unit, to show its contents in the right details pane.

6. Right-click the **Atlanta** organizational unit, select **New**, and then click **User**.

7. In the New Object – User window, enter **Office Staff Template** in the Full name text box.

8. In the User logon name text box, enter **OfficeStaffTemplate**.

9. Click **Next**.

10. In the Password and Confirm password text boxes, enter **Password01**.

11. Check the check box next to **Account is disabled**.

> It is not necessary to disable the template account, but it is a good security practice to do so.
>
> **NOTE**

12. Click **Next**.

13. Click **Finish**.

14. In the right details pane, right-click **Office Staff Template** and then click **Properties**.

15. Click the **Account** tab.

16. Click **Logon Hours**.

17. Set the account so users can only log on Monday through Friday, and then click **OK**.

18. Click the **Organization** tab.

19. In the Title text box, enter **Staff Member Title**.

20. In the Department text box, enter **Business Office**.

21. In the Company text box, enter **Super Management Corporation**.

22. Click **OK**.

23. In the right details pane, right-click **Office Staff Template** and then click **Copy**.

> You can use the Copy command on any user account, not only ones that you specifically use as templates.
>
> **TIP**

24. In the Full name text box, enter **Joe Noname XX** (where *XX* is the number of your server).

25. In the User logon name text box, enter **jnonameXX** (where *XX* is the number of your server).

26. Click **Next**.

27. In the Password and Confirm password text boxes, enter **Password01**.

28. Uncheck the check box next to **Account is disabled**.

29. Click **Next**.

30. Click **Finish**.

10

31. In the right details pane, right-click **Joe Noname XX** and then click **Properties**.

32. Click the **Organization** tab. Note the information from the Office Staff Template account that has been copied to Joe's new user account, as shown in Figure 10-1. Because the Title attribute of a user account is not marked as "Attribute is copied when duplicating user" in the Active Directory schema, that attribute was not copied.

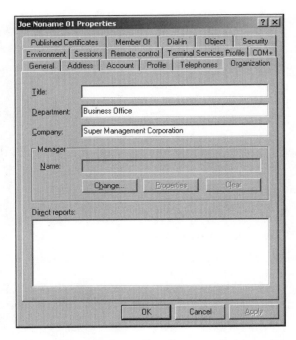

Figure 10-1 Information from copied template account

 Remember that not all attributes of a user account are copied when you copy a user account.

NOTE

33. If you wish, review the account's logon hours. When finished, click **OK** to close the account properties window.

34. Close Active Directory Users and Computers.

35. Log off your server if you do not intend to continue immediately to the next project. Otherwise, stay logged on.

Certification Objectives

Objectives for Microsoft Exam #70-294: Planning, Implementing, and Maintaining a Microsoft Windows Server 2003 Active Directory Infrastructure:

- Manage an Active Directory forest and domain structure.

REVIEW QUESTIONS

1. To create a template account, you must do which of the following?

   a. Check the "Make this a template account" check box when creating the account.

   b. From the New menu, select "Template" rather than "User."

   c. Right-click the account and then choose "Make template" after the user account is created.

   d. You do not have to do anything special; a template account is just a regular user account.

2. Which of the following attributes are not copied by default?

   a. Title

   b. Department

   c. Company

   d. All of the above are copied by default.

3. In order for a specific attribute of a user account to be copied, which of the following attribute options must be selected in the Active Directory schema?

   a. Attribute can be copied when duplicating.

   b. Attribute is copied when duplicating user.

   c. Attribute is duplicated when duplicating.

   d. There is no option to set which attributes are copied.

4. When creating a new account from the template, all attributes of the template account are copied. True or False?

5. For security reasons, it is a good idea to disable template accounts. True or False?

10

LAB 10.2 EXPORTING ACTIVE DIRECTORY USER ACCOUNTS USING CSVDE

Objectives

The goal of this lab is to learn how to use CSVDE to export user account data from Active Directory.

Materials Required

This lab will require the following:

- A Windows Server 2003 setup, as directed at the front of this lab manual

Estimated completion time: **5 minutes**

Activity Background

The CSVDE utility is useful for exporting data about the directory into comma-separated value files. The files CSVDE exports can easily be opened in a program like Microsoft Excel or imported into a database such as Microsoft Access or Microsoft SQL Server. In this lab, you will learn how to export information about all the user accounts in an organizational unit.

ACTIVITY

Activity

1. If necessary, start your server and log on using the **Administrator** account in the **CHILDXX** domain (where *XX* is the number of the forest root domain for which your server is a domain controller) using the password **Password01**.

2. Click **Start** and then click **Command Prompt**.

3. Type **CSVDE –f D:\CSVOUTXX.CSV –d "OU=Atlanta,OU= North America XX,DC=childZZ,DC=supercorp,DC=net" –r "(objectClass=user)"** (where *XX* is the number of your server and *ZZ* is the number of the forest root domain for which your server is a domain controller) and then press **Enter**. Be sure to type this command on one line, although it may wrap to the next line. Also, your instructor may provide you with an alternative path to save the output file if D: is not a hard drive. Note that information about the export process is displayed, as shown in Figure 10-2.

Figure 10-2   Exporting user account data using CSVDE

NOTE

You may have user accounts in addition to those shown in this lab's screen shots. By default, CSVDE exports objects in the container you specify and in all child containers. You can use the –p OneLevel parameter of the CSVDE command to export object data from the container you specify, and not from child containers. You can also use CSVDE -? to view help on all the parameters CSVDE supports.

4. Once the export completes, click **Start** and then click **My Computer**.

5. Double-click the **D:** drive. Alternatively, navigate to where you exported the file if your instructor provided an alternative path in Step 3.

6. Double-click the **CSVOUTXX** file (where *XX* is the number of your server) to open it. Notice that the file is in a comma-delimited format with the first row containing the column names, as shown in Figure 10-3.

Figure 10-3   CSVDE output of user account data

10

7. Close the file and then close the Windows Explorer window.

8. After answering the review questions, close the Command Prompt window.

9. Log off your server if you do not intend to continue immediately to the next project. Otherwise, stay logged on.

Certification Objectives

Objectives for Microsoft Exam #70-294: Planning, Implementing, and Maintaining a Microsoft Windows Server 2003 Active Directory Infrastructure:

- Manage an Active Directory forest and domain structure.

TIP

Use the help provided by CSVDE -? to answer the following questions.

REVIEW QUESTIONS

1. The _____ parameter of the CSVDE command specifies the input or output filename.

2. The _____ parameter of the CSVDE command specifies the root of the LDAP search.

3. You can use the _____ parameter of the CSVDE command to specify an LDAP search filter, such as "(objectClass=user)".

4. Which of the following parameters of the CSVDE command can be used to restrict a search to a single container?

   a. –s OneLevel

   b. –s CurrentContainer

   c. –p OneLevel

   d. –p CurrentContainer

5. In which of the following formats does CSVDE export data?

   a. in fixed column format

   b. in comma–delimited format

   c. in LDAP Data Interchange Format

   d. none of the above

LAB 10.3 IMPORTING ACTIVE DIRECTORY USER ACCOUNTS USING CSVDE

Objectives

The goal of this lab is to learn how to use CSVDE to import user account data from Active Directory. Note that due to the complexity of changing the domain's password policy, completing this lab is optional. You may also choose to complete Chapter 11 and then return to this lab at a later time.

Materials Required

This lab will require the following:

- A Windows Server 2003 setup, as directed at the front of this lab manual

Estimated completion time: **10 minutes**

Activity Background

You can use the CSVDE utility to create new objects in the directory, such as user accounts. However, one limitation to the CSVDE utility is that you can only create new user accounts that have blank passwords. By default, the Windows Server 2003 password policy requires that passwords be a minimum length and complexity. In order to complete this lab, you will need to modify the default password policy to allow blank passwords. Chapter 11 in the main text associated with this lab manual covers how to change a domain's password policy. Note that changing your password policy in a production environment just to use CVSDE is not recommended. Instead, you should use another tool such as DSADD or LDIFDE when your password policy requires passwords that are not blank.

To change a domain's password policy to accept blank passwords, click Start, select Administrative Tools, and then click Domain Security Policy. In the left tree pane, expand Account Policies and then select Password Policy. In the right details pane, double-click Minimum password length, set the number of characters to 0, and then click OK. In the right details pane, double-click Password must meet complexity requirements, select the Disabled option, click OK, and then close the Domain Security Policy. Note that these steps should only be performed on one server of a student group. Once you and your partner have both completed this lab, be sure to set the password policy back to its defaults (minimum of seven characters and require complex passwords).

TIP

After changing a domain's password policy, it may take several minutes for the changes to replicate and become active. So you do not have to wait, you can manually initiate replication using Active Directory Sites and Services. After both domain controllers in your student group have replicated, you can then run GPUPDATE on both servers to apply the new password policy.

10

ACTIVITY

Activity

1. If necessary, start your server and log on using the **Administrator** account in the **CHILDXX** domain (where *XX* is the number of the forest root domain for which your server is a domain controller) using the password **Password01**.

2. Click **Start**, select **All Programs**, select **Accessories**, and then click **Notepad**.

3. On the first line of the file, type (all on one line):

   DN,objectClass,sAMAccountName,userPrincipalName, displayName,userAccountControl

   These are the column headings that are required by CSVDE to create a new user account. The exact order of columns is not important as long as it is consistent from line to line. Each column should be separated by a comma. The following is a description of each column:

   - DN—Distinguished name of the new user.
   - objectClass—The name of the class from which a new object will be created.
   - sAMAccountName—The user's logon name (pre-Windows 2000).
   - userPrincipalName—The user's logon name (UPN).
   - displayName—The friendly user name that is shown in applications such as Microsoft Exchange.
   - userAccountControl—Used to control the status of an account. A value of 512 enables the user account and a value of 514 disables the account.

4. On the second line of the file, type (all on one line):

   "cn=CSVuser*XX*,ou=Atlanta,ou=North America *XX*,dc= child*ZZ*,dc=supercorp,dc=net",user,CSVuser*XX*, CSVuser*XX*@supercorp*XX*.com,CSV User *XX*,512

   Substitute *XX* for the number of your server and *ZZ* for the number of the forest root domain for which your server is a domain controller. Your file should now look similar to Figure10-4. Note that you can import more than one user at a time by putting each new account on its own line.

Figure 10-4   CSV file that creates a new user

5. On the File menu, click **Save**.

6. In the Save in drop-down list box, choose the **D:** drive. If you do not have a D: drive on your server, your instructor may provide you with an alternative path.

7. In the File name drop-down combo box, enter **CSVINXX.CSV** (where *XX* is the number of your server).

8. In the Save as type drop-down list box, select **All Files**.

9. Click **Save**.

10. Close **Notepad**.

11. Click **Start** and then click **Command Prompt**.

12. Type **CSVDE –i –f D:\CSVINXX.CSV** (where *XX* is the number of your server) and then press **Enter**. If successful, you should receive a message similar to the one shown in Figure 10-5.

```
Command Prompt                                              _ □ X
Microsoft Windows [Version 5.2.3790]
(C) Copyright 1985-2003 Microsoft Corp.

C:\>CSVDE -i -f D:\CSVIN01.CSV
Connecting to "(null)"
Logging in as current user using SSPI
Importing directory from file "D:\CSVIN01.CSV"
Loading entries..
1 entry modified successfully.

The command has completed successfully

C:\>_
```

Figure 10-5   Importing data using CSVDE

NOTE

If you receive an error that the password could not be updated, see the notes at the beginning of this lab.

13. Type **Exit** and press **Enter** to close the Command Prompt window.

14. Use Active Directory Users and Computers to confirm that the new account has been created in your Atlanta organizational unit.

15. Log off your server if you do not intend to continue immediately to the next project. Otherwise, stay logged on.

10

Certification Objectives

Objectives for Microsoft Exam #70-294: Planning, Implementing, and Maintaining a Microsoft Windows Server 2003 Active Directory Infrastructure:

- Manage an Active Directory forest and domain structure.

 Use the help provided by CSVDE -? to answer the following questions.

REVIEW QUESTIONS

1. The _____ parameter of the CSVDE command specifies that you want to run the command in import mode.

2. The sAMAccountName attribute specifies which of the following?

    a. A user's logon name (pre–Windows 2000)

    b. A user's logon name (UPN)

    c. A user's display name

    d. A user's distinguished name

3. You cannot use the CSVDE utility to modify an existing user account. True or False?

4. Which of the following is the default mode of the CSVDE command?

    a. Import

    b. Export

    c. It depends if a file name is specified or not.

    d. You must always explicitly specify the mode.

5. The CSVDE utility can set the password of a new user account. True or False?

LAB 10.4 CREATING GROUPS USING DSADD

Objectives

The goal of this lab is to learn how to use DSADD to create groups.

Materials Required

This lab will require the following:

- A Windows Server 2003 setup, as directed at the front of this lab manual

Estimated completion time: **5 minutes**

Activity Background

In Chapter 5, you learned how to use the DSADD command-line utility to add organizational units. In this lab, you will learn how to use DSADD to add groups. While this lab explicitly looks at using DSADD to work with groups, keep in mind that you can also use DSADD to work with a variety of other directory objects, such as users.

ACTIVITY

Activity

1. If necessary, start your server and log on using the **Administrator** account in the **CHILDXX** domain (where XX is the number of the forest root domain for which your server is a domain controller) using the password **Password01**.

2. Click **Start** and then click **Command Prompt**.

10

3. Type **DSADD GROUP "CN=Archive Readers _XX_,OU=Atlanta,OU= North America _XX_,DC=child_ZZ_,DC=supercorp,DC=net" –secgrp yes –scope 1** (where _XX_ is the number of your server and _ZZ_ is the number of the forest root domain for which your server is a domain controller) and then press **Enter**. Be sure to type the command on one line, although it may wrap to the next line. Notice that you are informed of the command's success or failure, as shown in Figure 10-6.

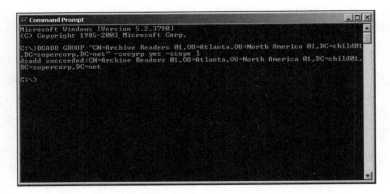

Figure 10-6   Using DSADD to create a new group

NOTE

You can use the -members and -memberOf parameters to specify who is a member of the group being created, and of what groups the new group is a member. You can give both parameters one or more distinguished names, separated by spaces.

4. Click **Start**, select **Administrative Tools**, and then click **Active Directory Users and Computers**.

5. Expand the necessary containers to locate the group you created in Step 3. Confirm that the group was created successfully. If the group does not appear or DSADD returned an error, confirm that the command was entered correctly and try again.

6. Close Active Directory Users and Computers.

7. After answering the review questions, close the Command Prompt window.

8. Log off your server if you do not intend to continue immediately to the next project. Otherwise, stay logged on.

Certification Objectives

Objectives for Microsoft Exam #70-294: Planning, Implementing, and Maintaining a Microsoft Windows Server 2003 Active Directory Infrastructure:

■ Manage an Active Directory forest and domain structure.

Use the help provided by DSADD GROUP /? to answer the following questions.

TIP

REVIEW QUESTIONS

1. You can use the _____ parameter of the DSADD GROUP command to add members to a group when creating the group.

2. You can use the _____ parameter of the DSADD GROUP command to add the new group as a member to existing groups when creating the new group.

3. To specify the global group scope, the letter _____ should follow the – scope parameter.

4. When using DSADD GROUP, if you do not specify whether or not the group is a security group, what will happen?

   a. A distribution group will be assumed and created.

   b. A security group will be assumed and created.

   c. You will be prompted to specify the group type.

   d. The command will return an error.

5. To specify multiple members when using the –members parameter of the DSADD GROUP command, you must separate the member's distinguished names with which of the following?

   a. a space ( )

   b. a comma (,)

   c. a vertical bracket (|)

   d. a plus sign (+)

10

Lab 10.5 Modifying Groups Using DSMOD

Objectives

The goal of this lab is to learn how to use DSMOD to modify groups.

Materials Required

This lab will require the following:

- A Windows Server 2003 setup, as directed at the front of this lab manual

Estimated completion time: **5 minutes**

Activity Background

In previous lab exercises, you have learned about the DSQUERY, DSGET, DSADD, DSMOVE, and DSRM command-line utilities. In this lab, you will learn about the last command in this group of six utilities: DSMOD. While this lab explicitly looks at using DSMOD to work with groups, keep in mind that you can also use DSMOD to work with a variety of other directory objects, such as users and organizational units.

ACTIVITY

Activity

1. If necessary, start your server and log on using the **Administrator** account in the **CHILDXX** domain (where XX is the number of the forest root domain for which your server is a domain controller) using the password **Password01**.

2. Click **Start** and then click **Command Prompt**.

3. Type **DSMOD GROUP "CN=Archive Readers XX,OU=Atlanta,OU= North America XX,DC=childZZ,DC=supercorp,DC=net" –addmbr "CN=Marketing Users XX,OU=Atlanta,OU=North America XX,DC=childZZ,DC=supercorp,DC=net"** (where *XX* is the number of your server and *ZZ* is the number of the forest root domain for which your server is a domain controller) and then press **Enter**. Be sure to type the command on one line, although it may wrap to the next line. Note that you are informed of the command's success or failure, as shown in Figure 10-7.

Figure 10-7   Using DSMOD to modify an existing group

10

4. Click **Start**, select **Administrative Tools**, and then click **Active Directory Users and Computers**.

5. Expand the necessary containers to locate the Archive Readers *XX* group (where *XX* is the number of your server) that you created in the last lab.

6. Right-click the **Archive Readers XX** group (where *XX* is the number of your server) and then click **Properties**.

7. Click the **Members** tab. Note that the Marketing Users *XX* group has been added to the Archive Readers group, as shown in Figure 10-8.

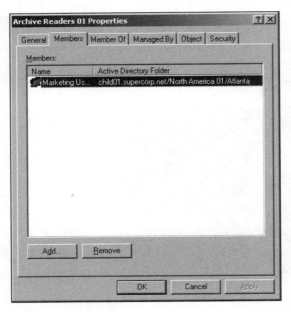

Figure 10-8   Results of adding group using DSMOD command

8. Click **OK**.

9. Close Active Directory Users and Computers.

10. After answering the review questions, close the Command Prompt window.

11. Log off your server.

Certification Objectives

Objectives for Microsoft Exam #70-294: Planning, Implementing, and Maintaining a Microsoft Windows Server 2003 Active Directory Infrastructure:

■ Manage an Active Directory forest and domain structure.

Use the help provided by DSMOD GROUP /? to answer the following questions.

TIP

REVIEW QUESTIONS

1. You can use the _____ parameter of the DSMOD GROUP command to remove members from a group.

2. You can use the _____ parameter of the DSMOD GROUP command to completely change (replace) the list of group members.

3. You can use the _____ parameter of the DSMOD GROUP command to change the group type.

4. You can use the _____ parameter of the DSMOD GROUP command to change the group scope.

5. You can modify more than one group at a time using DSMOD GROUP. True or False?

10

11

GROUP POLICY FOR CORPORATE POLICY

Labs included in this chapter:

♦ Lab 11.1 Configuring Account Lockout Policy Settings

♦ Lab 11.2 Configuring Service Settings Using Group Policy

♦ Lab 11.3 Configuring Security Option Settings Using Group Policy

♦ Lab 11.4 Assigning Login Scripts to Users Using Group Policy

♦ Lab 11.5 Determining Group Policy Settings Using GPRESULT

Microsoft MCSE Exam #70-294 Objectives	
Objective	Lab
Configure the user environment by using Group Policy.	11.4
Deploy a computer environment by using Group Policy.	11.1, 11.2, 11.3
Troubleshoot issues related to Group Policy application deployment.	11.5
Troubleshoot the application of Group Policy security settings.	11.5

LAB 11.1 CONFIGURING ACCOUNT LOCKOUT POLICY SETTINGS

Objectives

The goal of this lab is to learn how to configure an account lockout policy.

Because these settings must be set at the domain level, you and your partner should work as a team, performing these steps on only one of your servers.

Materials Required

This lab will require the following:

- A Windows Server 2003 setup, as directed at the front of this lab manual

Estimated completion time: **10 minutes**

Activity Background

In order to prevent someone from endlessly guessing passwords, an administrator can configure an account lockout policy for the domain. The Account lockout threshold policy determines how many failed logon attempts can occur before an account is locked out. The Reset account lockout counter policy defines how long to wait before the failed logon attempt counter is reset to zero. Finally, the Account lockout duration policy specifies how long an account should remain locked out once the Account lockout threshold is reached. Remember that the account lockout policy must be set at the domain level to affect domain accounts.

Activity

1. If necessary, start your server and log on using the **Administrator** account in the **CHILDXX** domain (where *XX* is the number of the forest root domain for which your server is a domain controller) using the password **Password01**.

2. Click **Start**, select **Administrative Tools**, and then click **Active Directory Users and Computers**.

3. In the left tree pane, right-click **ChildXX.supercorp.net** (where *XX* is the number of the forest root domain for which your server is a domain controller) and then click **Properties**.

4. Click the **Group Policy** tab, ensure that Default Domain Policy is selected, and then click **Edit**. Alternatively, if you have installed the Group Policy Management Console (GPMC), click **Open** to open the GPMC, right-click the **Default Domain Policy** GPO link, and then click **Edit**.

5. In the left tree pane under the Computer Configuration section, expand **Windows Settings**, **Security Settings**, and then **Account Policies**.

6. In the left tree pane, click **Account Lockout Policy** to view the available policies in the right details pane, as shown in Figure 11-1.

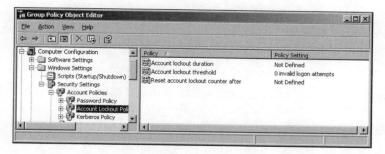

Figure 11-1   Account Lockout Policy node of a Group Policy object

7. In the right details pane, double-click **Account lockout threshold**.

8. Confirm that the Define this policy setting checkbox is checked.

9. Set the Account will lock out after spin box to **10**, as shown in Figure 11-2, and then click **OK**. This will allow up to 10 invalid logon attempts before an account is locked out.

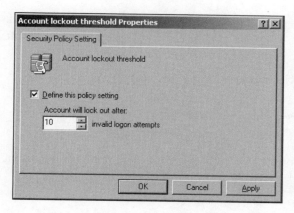

Figure 11-2   Configuring the account lockout threshold

11

In a production environment, it is recommended that accounts be locked out after 3 to 5 invalid logon attempts. Setting the Account lockout threshold higher than this recommended value should only be done in isolated testing environments that do not contain sensitive data.

10. The Suggested Value Changes window appears. Click **OK**. Note that, in addition to the Account lockout threshold policy, the Account lockout duration and Reset account lockout counter after policies have also been changed.

11. In the right details pane, double-click **Account lockout duration**.

12. Set the Account is locked out for spin box to **5** and then click **OK**. In the event an account is locked out, the account will now automatically be unlocked after 5 minutes.

13. The Suggested Value Changes window will appear. Click **OK**. The Reset account lockout counter after policy defines how much time must pass from the first invalid logon attempt before the counter is reset.

14. Close the Group Policy Object Editor console.

15. Close all other open windows.

16. Log off your server if you do not intend to continue immediately to the next project. Otherwise, stay logged on.

Certification Objectives

Objectives for Microsoft Exam #70-294: Planning, Implementing, and Maintaining a Microsoft Windows Server 2003 Active Directory Infrastructure:

■ Deploy a computer environment by using Group Policy.

REVIEW QUESTIONS

1. To affect domain accounts, you can set account lockout settings at which of the following levels?

   a. only at the domain level

   b. at the domain level or on the domain controller organizational unit

   c. at the domain level or any organizational unit

   d. at any level for which Group Policy can be applied

2. You cannot configure account lockout settings in the User Configuration section of Group Policy. True or False?

3. Which of the following defines how many invalid logon attempts can occur before an account is locked out?

   a. Account lockout duration

   b. Account lockout threshold

   c. Reset account lockout counter after

   d. Reset locked-out account after

4. Which of the following defines how much time must pass before a locked-out account is automatically unlocked?

   a. Account lockout duration

   b. Account lockout threshold

   c. Reset account lockout counter after

   d. Reset locked-out account after

5. Which of the following defines how much time must pass before the invalid logon attempts counter is reset?

   a. Account lockout duration

   b. Account lockout threshold

   c. Reset account lockout counter after

   d. Reset locked-out account after

11

LAB 11.2 CONFIGURING SERVICE SETTINGS USING GROUP POLICY

Objectives

The goal of this lab is to learn how you can use Group Policy to configure service settings.

Materials Required

This lab will require the following:

- A Windows Server 2003 setup, as directed at the front of this lab manual

Estimated completion time: **10 minutes**

Activity Background

One of the first steps you can take to secure a network is to disable any unnecessary services. To simplify management—and ensure that services that are disabled stay disabled—you can use Group Policy to configure a service's startup parameters. In this lab, you will learn how to disable unnecessary services using Group Policy.

ACTIVITY

Activity

1. If necessary, start your server and log on using the **Administrator** account in the **CHILD*XX*** domain (where *XX* is the number of the forest root domain for which your server is a domain controller) using the password **Password01**.

2. Click **Start**, select **Administrative Tools**, and then click **Active Directory Sites and Services**.

3. If necessary, in the left tree pane, expand the **Sites** folder.

4. In the left tree pane, right-click **MySite*XX*** (where *XX* is the number of your server) and then click **Properties**.

5. Click the **Group Policy** tab.

6. Click **New** to create a new GPO and name it **Service Restrictions XX** (where *XX* is the number of your server). Alternatively, if you have installed the GPMC, click **Open** to open the console and then create and link a new GPO to your MySite*XX* site.

TIP

When using the GPMC, remember that a GPO exists in a single domain, but can be linked to multiple locations throughout the forest. When you want to create a new GPO that is linked to a site, you must first create the GPO in one of the forest's domains and then link it to the site. You can create a new GPO in the GPMC by right-clicking the Group Policy Objects folder under the desired domain (which is Child*XX*.supercorp.net for this lab) and then clicking New. You can then link the new GPO to the site by right-clicking the site in the left tree pane and selecting Link an Existing GPO.

7. Right-click the **GPO** you have just created and then click **Edit**.

8. In the left tree pane, under Computer Configuration, expand **Windows Settings** and then **Security Settings**.

9. In the left tree pane, click **System Services** to show a list of services in the right details pane, as shown in Figure 11-3.

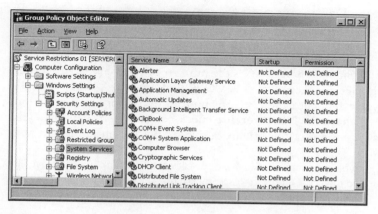

Figure 11-3   System Services node of a Group Policy object

10. In the right details pane, right-click **ClipBook** and then click **Properties**.

11. Check the **Define this policy setting** check box, and confirm that Disabled is selected, as shown in Figure 11-4.

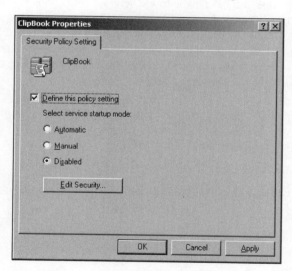

Figure 11-4   Configuring the properties of the ClipBook service

12. Click the **Edit Security** button, and review the security settings assigned to the Administrators group. These permissions control how administrators can interact with this service after the policy settings are applied. Click **Cancel** when finished to discard any accidental changes.

13. Click **OK** to close the ClipBook Properties window.

14. In the right details pane, scroll down and right-click **Routing and Remote Access** and then click **Properties**.

15. Check the **Define this policy setting** check box, confirm that Disabled is selected, and then click **OK**.

16. Close the Group Policy Object Editor window.

17. In the MySite*XX* (where *XX* is the number of your server) Properties window, with the Service Restrictions *XX* GPO link (where *XX* is the number of your server) selected, click the **Options** button. In the Service Restrictions Options window, check the **No Override** check box and then click **OK**. This will stop policies applied after this one from overriding the settings in this policy.

If you are using the GPMC, right-click the GPO link under the MySite*XX* site and then click Enforced to accomplish the same as Step 17—but using the GPMC. Close the GPMC when finished. When prompted to confirm the change, click OK.

18. Click **Close** to close the MySite*XX* properties window.

Because the Group Policy Object Editor attempts to connect to the PDC emulator by default, and because your and your partner's servers are not located in the same site, the changes you have made to the Services Restrictions *XX* policy were made on the PDC emulator, but have probably not yet replicated to the second domain controller in your domain. To continue with this project, if your server is not the PDC emulator for the domain (which should be the student with the higher server number), manually initiate replication from your partner's server before closing Active Directory Users and Computers.

19. Close Active Directory Sites and Services.

20. Click **Start** and then click **Command Prompt**.

21. Type **GPUPDATE** and then press **Enter** to refresh Group Policy.

22. Type **Exit** and press **Enter** to close the Command Prompt window.

23. Click **Start**, select **Administrative Tools**, and then click **Services**. The Services console is shown in Figure 11-5.

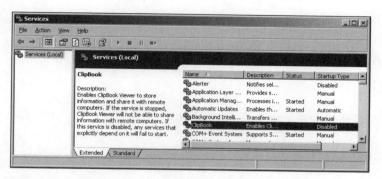

Figure 11-5 Viewing service settings after the application of a Group Policy object

24. Review the Startup Type column settings for both the ClipBook and Routing and Remote Access Service services, confirming that they are both now set to Disabled.

25. Close the Services console.

26. Log off your server if you do not intend to continue immediately to the next project. Otherwise, stay logged on.

Certification Objectives

Objectives for Microsoft Exam #70-294: Planning, Implementing, and Maintaining a Microsoft Windows Server 2003 Active Directory Infrastructure:

- Deploy a computer environment by using Group Policy.

REVIEW QUESTIONS

1. Service configuration settings are found under which of the following nodes of the Computer Configuration section of a Group Policy object?

   a. Computer Configuration > Windows Settings > Security Settings

   b. User Configuration > Windows Settings > Security Settings

   c. Computer Configuration > Administrative Templates

   d. User Configuration > Administrative Templates

2. You can configure System Service settings in Group Policy objects applied to which of the following? (Choose all that apply.)

   a. Local Computer

   b. Domain

   c. Site

   d. OU

3. To configure service security settings using Group Policy, click the _____ button after defining the policy setting.

4. When Group Policy settings are applied at the site level with the No Override option, they cannot be overridden at the domain or organizational unit level. True or False?

5. You cannot configure service settings in the User Configuration section of Group Policy. True or False?

LAB 11.3 CONFIGURING SECURITY OPTION SETTINGS USING GROUP POLICY

Objectives

The goal of this lab is to learn how to configure a logon message on domain computers. The message you enter will appear each time a user attempts to log on to a computer affected by the policy.

Materials Required

This lab will require the following:

- A Windows Server 2003 setup, as directed at the front of this lab manual

Estimated completion time: **10 minutes**

Activity Background

Some organizations have legal requirements or notices about which they may want to remind their network users. One policy, called Interactive logon: Message text for users attempting to log on, can help in this situation. When configured, users are prompted with the message defined in the policy. Users must click OK before the logon process can continue.

Activity

1. If necessary, start your server and log on using the **Administrator** account in the **CHILDXX** domain (where *XX* is the number of the forest root domain for which your server is a domain controller) using the password **Password01**.

2. Click **Start**, select **Administrative Tools**, and then click **Active Directory Users and Computers**.

3. In the left tree pane, right-click the **North America XX** organizational unit (where *XX* is the number of your server) and then click **Properties**.

4. Click the **Group Policy** tab, right-click the **Desktop Preferences XX** GPO link (where *XX* is the number of your server), and then click **Edit**. Alternatively, if you have installed the GPMC, click **Open** to open the GPMC, right-click the **Desktop Preferences XX** GPO link (where *XX* is the number of your server), and then click **Edit**.

5. In the left tree pane, under Computer Configuration, expand **Windows Settings**, **Security Settings**, and then **Local Policies**.

6. In the left tree pane, click **Security Options** to view a list of available settings in the right details pane.

7. Double-click **Interactive logon: Message text for users attempting to log on** in the right details pane.

8. Check the **Define this policy setting in the template** check box. In the text box, type **Only Authorized Users of Super Corporation are permitted to use this system**, as shown in Figure 11-6, and then click OK.

11

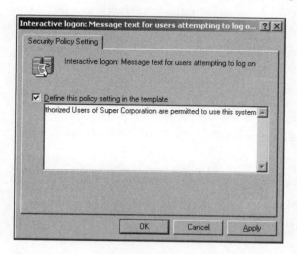

Figure 11-6   Setting interactive logon message text

9. Double-click **Interactive logon: Message title for users attempting to log on** in the right details pane.

10. Check the **Define this policy setting** checkbox. In the text box, type **Super Corporation Security Policy**, as shown in Figure 11-7, and then click **OK**.

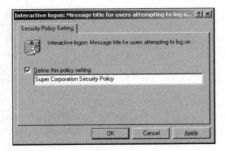

Figure 11-7 Setting interactive logon message title

11. Close the Group Policy Object Editor console. Any computer affected by the group policy you have created will now display the message you entered when a user attempts to log on.

12. Close all other open windows.

13. Log off your server if you do not intend to continue immediately to the next project. Otherwise, stay logged on.

Certification Objectives

Objectives for Microsoft Exam #70-294: Planning, Implementing, and Maintaining a Microsoft Windows Server 2003 Active Directory Infrastructure:

- Deploy a computer environment by using Group Policy.

REVIEW QUESTIONS

1. You can set security option settings at which of the following levels?

a. only at the domain level

b. at the domain level or on the domain controller organizational unit

c. at the domain level or any organizational unit

d. at any level to which Group Policy can be applied

2. Security option settings are found under which of the following nodes of the Computer Configuration section of a Group Policy object? (Choose all that apply.)

    a. Computer Configuration > Windows Settings > Security Settings

    b. User Configuration > Windows Settings > Security Settings

    c. Computer Configuration > Administrative Templates

    d. User Configuration > Administrative Templates

3. A security option is available to disable the display of the last user who logged on to a computer. True or False?

4. At a command prompt, you can run the _____ command to refresh the security option settings applied by Group Policy.

5. You cannot configure security option settings in the User Configuration section of Group Policy. True or False?

LAB 11.4 ASSIGNING LOGIN SCRIPTS TO USERS USING GROUP POLICY

Objectives

The goal of this lab is to learn how to use Group Policy to assign logon scripts to domain users.

11

Materials Required

This lab will require the following:

- A Windows Server 2003 setup, as directed at the front of this lab manual

Estimated completion time: **10 minutes**

Activity Background

While Group Policy is extremely flexible, it still can't do everything. However, by using a script and assigning it through Group Policy, you can do just about anything. In this lab, you will learn how to assign a logon script to users using Group Policy.

ACTIVITY

Activity

1. If necessary, start your server and log on using the **Administrator** account in the **CHILDXX** domain (where *XX* is the number of the forest root domain for which your server is a domain controller) using the password **Password01**.

2. Click **Start**, select **Administrative Tools**, and then click **Active Directory Users and Computers**.

3. In the left tree pane, right-click the **North America XX** organizational unit (where *XX* is the number of your server) and then click **Properties**.

4. Click the **Group Policy** tab, right-click the **Desktop Preferences XX** GPO link (where *XX* is the number of your server), and then click **Edit**. Alternatively, if you have installed the GPMC, click **Open** to open the GPMC, right-click the **Desktop Preferences XX** GPO link (where *XX* is the number of your server), and then click **Edit**.

5. In the left tree pane, under User Configuration, expand **Windows Settings**.

6. In the left tree pane, click **Scripts (Logon/Logoff)**.

7. In the right details pane, double-click **Logon** and then click **Show Files**. Note the path of the folder that is opened.

8. On the **Tools** menu, click **Folder Options**, and then click the **View** tab.

9. In the Advanced settings section, confirm that the Hide extensions for known file types check box is unchecked, and then click **OK**.

10. On the **File** menu, select **New**, and then click **Text Document**. If the file does not appear immediately, you may need to click **Refresh** on the View menu.

11. Double-click the **New Text Document.txt** file to open it.

12. On the first line of the file, type **NET USE X: \\SERVERXX\SYSVOL** (where *XX* is the number of your server). Save the file and then close it. The NET USE command in this example maps the X: drive to the SYSVOL share on your server.

13. Right-click **New Text Document.txt** and click **Rename**. Type **logon.bat** and then press **Enter**, as shown in Figure 11-8. When prompted to confirm whether you want to change the file's extension, click **Yes**. Again, if the file's new name does not immediately appear, you may need to click **Refresh** on the View menu.

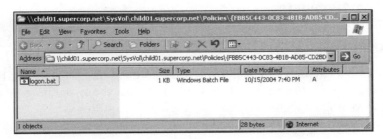

Figure 11-8   Creating a new batch file for use as a logon script

14. Close the Explorer window.

15. In the Logon Properties window, click **Add**. In the Add a Script window, click **Browse** and then double-click **logon.bat**. Click **OK** to close the Add a script window, and then click **OK** again to close the Logon Properties window shown in Figure 11-9.

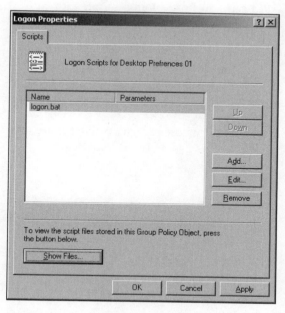

Figure 11-9   Adding a user logon script to a Group Policy object

16. Close all other open windows.

17. Log off your server if you do not intend to continue immediately to the next project. Otherwise, stay logged on.

Certification Objectives

Objectives for Microsoft Exam #70-294: Planning, Implementing, and Maintaining a Microsoft Windows Server 2003 Active Directory Infrastructure:

■ Configure the user environment by using Group Policy.

REVIEW QUESTIONS

1. In which portion of a GPO can you store a logon script?

   a. Group policy container (GPC)

   b. Group policy template (GPT)

   c. Both the GPC and the GPT

   d. Neither the GPC nor the GPT

2. When a logon or logoff script runs, whose security privileges are used?

   a. the local system's

   b. the user's

   c. the domain's

   d. none of the above

3. When a startup or shutdown script runs, whose security privileges are used?

   a. the local system's

   b. the user's

   c. the domain's

   d. none of the above

4. Which of the following file types can be used as logon scripts? (Choose all that apply.)

   a. .bat

   b. .adm

   c. .vbs

   d. .txt

5. If a slow link is detected, logon scripts do not run by default. True or False?

LAB 11.5 DETERMINING GROUP POLICY SETTINGS USING GPRESULT

Objectives

The goal of this lab is to learn how you can gather Resultant Set of Policy (RSoP) data using the GPRESULT command-line utility.

Materials Required

This lab will require the following:

- A Windows Server 2003 setup, as directed at the front of this lab manual

Estimated completion time: **5 minutes**

Activity Background

While the RSoP snap-in can provide lots of detailed data, there may be times when you just need quick information about the policies in effect on a client workstation or server. In such situations, you can use the GPRESULT command to quickly find out what policies are in effect. While GPRESULT will not tell you from which GPO a particular policy came, the data provided by GPRESULT is still helpful.

ACTIVITY

Activity

1. If necessary, start your server and log on using the **Administrator** account in the **CHILDXX** domain (where *XX* is the number of the forest root domain for which your server is a domain controller) using the password **Password01**.

2. Click **Start** and then click **Command Prompt**.

3. At the command prompt, type **GPRESULT /?** and press **Enter**. Review the switches associated with the GPRESULT command and their purposes.

4. To view the Group Policy settings applied to the administrator user account, type **GPRESULT /user administrator** and press **Enter**.

5. Scroll through the output provided by the GPRESULT tool, as illustrated in Figure 11-10. Review the information provided by the GPRESULT command, including which policies are applied to the administrator user account.

11

Figure 11-10 Viewing the output of the GPRESULT tool

6. Type **Exit** and then press **Enter** to close the Command Prompt window.

7. Log off your server.

Certification Objectives

Objectives for Microsoft Exam #70-294: Planning, Implementing, and Maintaining a Microsoft Windows Server 2003 Active Directory Infrastructure:

- Troubleshoot issues related to Group Policy application deployment.

- Troubleshoot the application of Group Policy security settings.

REVIEW QUESTIONS

1. Which of the following are valid switches when using the GPRESULT command? (Choose all that apply.)

   a. /?

   b. /user

   c. /computer

   d. /system

2. Using the GPRESULT command, which of the following represents the correct syntax for determining the Group Policy settings applied to a user named John on the local computer?

   a. gpresult /u:john

   b. gpresult /user john

   c. gpresult –a:john

   d. gpresult /all

3. You can use the GPRESULT command to determine the Group Policy settings that will apply to a particular user on a different computer. True or False?

4. Using the GPRESULT command, which of the following represents the correct syntax for determining the Group Policy settings applied to a user named John on a computer named DESKTOP3?

   a. gpresult /user:john /computer:desktop3

   b. gpresult /user john /s desktop3

   c. gpresult /all

   d. gpresult /c:desktop3 user:john

5. Issuing the GPRESULT command with no parameters will retrieve RSoP information for the currently logged-on user. True or False?

12

DEPLOYING AND MANAGING SOFTWARE WITH GROUP POLICY

Labs included in this chapter:

♦ Lab 12.1 Creating a Custom MSI Package

♦ Lab 12.2 Assigning Software to Computers

♦ Lab 12.3 Modifying a Custom MSI Package

♦ Lab 12.4 Upgrading Deployed Software

Microsoft MCSE Exam #70-294 Objectives	
Objective	Lab
Configure the user environment by using Group Policy.	12.1, 12.3
Deploy a computer environment by using Group Policy.	12.1, 12.2, 12.3
Maintain installed software by using Group Policy.	12.4

Lab 12.1 Creating a Custom MSI Package

Objectives

The goal of this lab is to learn how to create custom MSI packages using WinINSTALL LE 2003.

Materials Required

This lab will require the following:

- A Windows Server 2003 setup, as directed at the front of this lab manual

- A connection to the Internet

Estimated completion time: **30 minutes**

Activity Background

When deploying software using Group Policy, your first choice should be to use an MSI provided by the application vendor. However, not all vendors supply MSI packages with their applications. In situations where you must create a custom MSI package for an application, tools such as WinINSTALL can be used. This lab will walk you through the steps required to create a custom MSI package for WinZip.

TIP

WinINSTALL works by taking a 'before' snapshot before the application is installed, an 'after' snapshot after the application is installed, and then comparing the two snapshots to determine what files and registry entries were added by the installation program. For the best results when using WinINSTALL, you should use a new installation of Windows with no other applications installed. Additionally, you should make the snapshots on the operating system on which the custom MSI will be installed. In other words, if the MSI will be installed on computers that primarily run Windows 2000 Professional, you should create the snapshots from a Windows 2000 Professional computer.

Activity

1. If necessary, start your server and log on using the **Administrator** account in the **CHILDXX** domain (where *XX* is the number of the forest root domain for which your server is a domain controller) using the password **Password01**.

> Your instructor may have already downloaded the files necessary for this lab for you. If so, follow the instructions provided by your instructor, rather than downloading the files. Also note that WinZip should not yet be installed on your server. If WinZip is already installed, you will need to use the Add or Remove Programs applet in the Control Panel to remove WinZip before continuing.
>
> **NOTE**

2. Click **Start**, select **All Programs**, and then click **Internet Explorer**.

> Web sites are frequently redesigned. You may need to modify the following steps in order to locate the download link for WinINSTALL LE 2003.
>
> **NOTE**

3. In the Address bar, type **www.ondemandsoftware.com** and then click **Go**.

4. Click the **Products** link on the left menu.

5. Under the heading Software Distribution System, click **WinINSTALL LE 2003**.

6. Locate the **Download WinINSTALL LE 2003 NOW!** link and click it.

7. When prompted to save or open the file, click **Open**.

8. If the Security Warning window appears, click **Yes**.

9. When the Welcome to the WinINSTALL LE 2003 Setup Wizard displays, click **Next**.

10. Click **Next** three times to view the Product Information windows.

11. Accept the License Agreement and then click **Next**.

12. In the E-mail Address text box, enter an e-mail address. If you do not have an e-mail address or do not wish to use your own e-mail address, you can create a free e-mail account at hotmail.com or yahoo.com.

13. Uncheck the check box next to **Sign me up for a free copy of WinINSTALL News**.

14. Click **Next**.

15. On the Custom Setup screen, click **Next**.

16. In the Share Name text box, enter **WinINSTALL** and then click **Next**. This share will allow you to run the WinINSTALL discover tool without having WinINSTALL installed on a system.

17. Click **Install**. When the installation finishes, click **Finish**.

12

18. In the Address bar of Internet Explorer, type **www.winzip.com** and then click **Go**.

19. On the left menu, click **WinZip** under the Downloads heading and then click **Download Evaluation**. You may need to search for the download link if the site has been reorganized.

20. Click the second **Download WinZip 8.1 SR-1** (download from a WinZip download server) link. If version 8.1 SR-1 is not available, choose the current version.

21. When prompted to save or open the file, click **Save**.

22. In the Save As dialog box, save the file to the root of the D: hard drive as **winzip.exe**. Your instructor may provide you with an alternative location if you do not have a hard drive labeled D:.

23. When the download completes, click **Close**.

24. Close Internet Explorer.

25. Click **Start**, and then click **Run**.

26. In the Run dialog box, enter **\\SERVERXX\WinINSTALL\Disco32.exe** (where *XX* is the number of your server) and then click **OK**.

The Disco32 application can be accessed over the network without the need to have WinINSTALL installed locally. This allows you to use a "fresh" installation of Windows (that is, just Windows installed with no other applications) when creating custom MSI packages.

27. If you are prompted to open the file, click **Open**.

28. In the Welcome to the Discover Wizard dialog box, click **Next**.

29. In the Specify the name of the application text box, enter **WinZip**.

30. Click the **...** button.

31. In the Look in drop-down list box, select **My Network Places**.

32. Double-click **Entire Network**, **Microsoft Windows Network**, **ChildXX** (where *XX* is the number of the forest root domain for which your server is a domain controller), **SERVERXX** (where *XX* is the number of your server), and then **Software**.

33. Click the **Create New Folder** icon (it is at the upper right and looks like a folder), and name the new folder **WinZip**.

34. Double-click the **WinZip** folder.

35. In the File name text box, enter **WinZip** and then click **Open**. Your screen should now look similar to Figure 12-1.

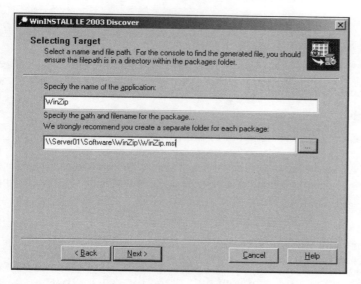

Figure 12-1   Specifying the new package name and location

36. Click **Next**.

37. Click **Next** to accept the default working drive.

38. In the Drive Selection dialog box, select the **[-C-]** drive in the Available Drives list box.

39. Click **Add** to move the [-C-] drive to the Drives to Scan list box, and then click **Next**.

40. Click **Next** to accept the default file exclusions.

41. Click **Next** to accept the default registry exclusions.

42. Click **Finish**. WinINSTALL Discover will create the Before snapshot by scanning the C: drive and registry.

43. When the Before snapshot is complete, click **OK**.

44. In the Look in drop-down list box, select the **D:** drive (or the location where you saved winzip.exe in step 22) and then double-click **winzip.exe**.

 These instructions are for WinZip version 8.1 SR-1. You may need to modify them slightly if you downloaded a different version.

NOTE

45. On the WinZip setup screen, click **Setup**.

46. Click **OK** to accept the default installation location.

47. In the features dialog box, click **Next**.

48. Click **Yes** to accept the license agreement.

49. In the Quick Start dialog box, click **Next**.

50. Select the **Start with WinZip Classic** option, and then click **Next**.

51. Confirm that the **Express setup** option is selected, and then click **Next**.

52. In the Associations dialog box, click **Next**.

53. Click **Finish**.

54. Click **Close** on the WinZip Tip of the Day and then close WinZip.

 NOTE If you wanted to customize the installation by adding/removing icons or configuring application defaults, you could do so at this point—before creating the After snapshot.

55. Click **Start**, and then click **Run**.

56. In the Run dialog box, enter **\\SERVERXX\WinINSTALL\Disco32.exe** (where *XX* is the number of your server) and then click **OK**.

57. If you are prompted to open the file, click **Open**.

58. In the Welcome to the Discover Wizard dialog box, confirm that the **Perform the 'After' snapshot now** option is selected, as shown in Figure 12-2, and then click **Next**. WinINSTALL Discover will create the After snapshot and compare it to the Before snapshot to create the custom MSI package.

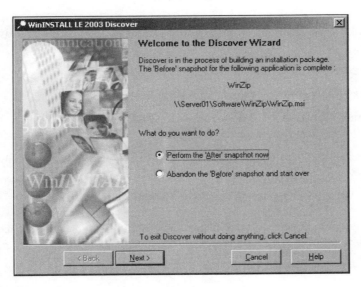

Figure 12-2 Creating the After snapshot

59. Once the process completes, any error or warning messages will be displayed. If you receive any warnings, read the warnings and then click **Close**.

60. A message box informs you that the package was created. Click **OK**.

61. You now have created an MSI package that you can use to install WinZip. So you can deploy the package on your server, you will now uninstall WinZip. Click **Start**, select **Control Panel**, and then click **Add or Remove Programs**.

> In a production environment, you should test the package on a computer that has not had WinZip installed on it first.
>
> **TIP**

62. In the Currently installed programs list box, select **WinZip** and then click **Change/Remove**.

63. Click **Yes** when asked if you are sure you want to continue.

64. Click **Yes** again when asked if you are sure you want to continue.

65. A message box informs you that the uninstall is complete. Click **OK**.

66. Close Add or Remove Programs.

67. Log off your server if you do not intend to continue immediately to the next project. Otherwise, stay logged on.

Certification Objectives

Objectives for Microsoft Exam #70-294: Planning, Implementing, and Maintaining a Microsoft Windows Server 2003 Active Directory Infrastructure:

- Configure the user environment by using Group Policy

- Deploy a computer environment by using Group Policy

12

REVIEW QUESTIONS

1. The WinINSTALL Discover tool works by which of the following?

   a. disassembling the .exe installation file of the application

   b. intercepting all commands from the installation to the operating system

   c. creating a Before and After snapshot of the registry and file system, and then comparing the two snapshots

   d. none of the above

2. When using the WinINSTALL Discover tool to create a package that will be deployed to all desktop users in the company, which of the following systems should you use to create the package?

   a. a domain controller running Windows Server 2003

   b. a member server running Windows Server 2003

   c. a Windows XP workstation containing all other software used by the company

   d. a Windows XP workstation that contains a newly installed copy of Windows

3. Using a custom .msi file is preferable to using a .msi file provided by the software publisher. True or False?

4. In order to use the WinINSTALL Discover tool on a system, WinINSTALL must be fully installed on that system first. True or False?

5. A custom .msi file is equivalent to a custom .zap file. True or False?

Lab 12.2 Assigning Software to Computers

Objectives

The goal of this lab is to learn how to deploy software to computers.

Materials Required

This lab will require the following:

- A Windows Server 2003 setup, as directed at the front of this lab manual

Estimated completion time: **15 minutes**

Activity Background

When using Group Policy, software can be deployed to users or computers. Deploying software to computers is useful when an application is used by everyone—not just a select set of users. In this activity, you will learn how to deploy software to computers using Group Policy.

Activity

1. If necessary, start your server and log on using the **Administrator** account in the **CHILDXX** domain (where *XX* is the number of the forest root domain for which your server is a domain controller) using the password **Password01**.

2. Click **Start**, select **Administrative Tools**, and then click **Active Directory Users and Computers**.

3. In the left tree pane, right-click the **Domain Controllers** organizational unit, select **New**, and then click **Organizational Unit**.

4. In the **Name** text box, enter **My Server XX** (where *XX* is the number of your server) and then click **OK**.

5. In the left tree pane, click the **Domain Controllers** organizational unit to show its contents in the right details pane.

6. In the right details pane, right-click **SERVERXX** (where *XX* is the number of your server) and then click **Move**.

7. In the Move dialog box, select the **My Server XX** organizational unit (where *XX* is the number of your server) under the Domain Controllers organizational unit, and then click **OK**.

8. In the right details pane, right-click the **My Server XX** organizational unit (where *XX* is the number of your server) and then click **Properties**.

9. Click the **Group Policy** tab.

10. If you do not have the GPMC installed, click **New** to create a new GPO and name it **My Server XX** (where *XX* is the number of your server) and then press **Enter**. Alternatively, if you have installed the GPMC, click **Open** to open the GPMC. Once the GPMC is opened, right-click the **My Server XX** organizational unit (where *XX* is the number of your server) and then click **Create and Link a GPO Here**. Name the new GPO **My Server XX** (where *XX* is the number of your server) and then click **OK**.

11. Right-click the **My Server XX** GPO link (where *XX* is the number of your server) and then click **Edit** to open the Group Policy Object Editor.

12. In the left tree pane, expand **Software Settings** under Computer Configuration.

13. Right-click **Software installation**, select **New**, and then click **Package**.

14. In the File name text box, enter **\\SERVERXX\Software\WinZip** (where *XX* is the number of your server) and then press **Enter**.

15. Double-click **WinZip.msi**.

12

16. In the Deploy Software dialog box, select Advanced, as shown in Figure 12-3, and then click **OK**.

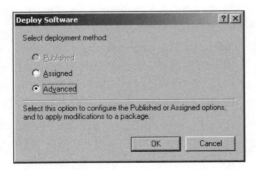

Figure 12-3   Selecting deployment method

17. Click the **Deployment** tab.

18. Check the check box next to **Uninstall this application when it falls out of the scope of management**, as shown in Figure 12-4, and then click OK.

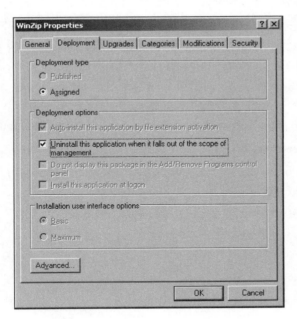

Figure 12-4   Setting deployment options

19. Close all open windows. If your partner is also performing this lab at the same time, wait for your partner to perform the previous steps before continuing.

NOTE Because all Group Policy changes are made on the PDC emulator by default, the changes to Group Policy will need to replicate to the other domain controller in your student domain. Before continuing, you should use Active Directory Sites and Services to initiate replication manually from your partner's server.

20. Restart your server. Notice that during the startup process, the message Installing managed software WinZip appears.

21. Log on using the **Administrator** account in the **CHILDXX** domain (where *XX* is the number of the forest root domain for which your server is a domain controller) using the password **Password01**.

22. Confirm that WinZip is installed and runs. Because WinZip settings are customized per user, the WinZip Configuration Wizard will run again. Note that the reason this setup runs is a function of WinZip and not Windows Installer or Group Policy.

23. Log off your server if you do not intend to continue immediately to the next project. Otherwise, stay logged on.

Certification Objectives

Objectives for Microsoft Exam #70-294: Planning, Implementing, and Maintaining a Microsoft Windows Server 2003 Active Directory Infrastructure:

- Deploy a computer environment by using Group Policy

12

REVIEW QUESTIONS

1. When deploying software to computers, which of the following methods are available?

   a. Assigning

   b. Publishing

   c. both Assigning and Publishing

   d. neither Assigning nor Publishing

2. When software is deployed to a computer, when is it installed?

   a. when the computer starts

   b. when the first user logs on

   c. when Group Policy refreshes

   d. when the computer starts and also before it shuts down

3. When deploying software, you should always use a universal naming convention (UNC) path, such as \\ServerName\Share, and not a local path. True or false?

4. When software is assigned to a computer, it is resilient against which of the following? (Choose all that apply.)

   a. corrupted files

   b. missing files

   c. misconfiguration

   d. uninstallation

5. Which of the following options would you select when you want software to be removed if a GPO no longer applies to the computer?

   a. Do not display this package in the Add/Remove Programs control panel

   b. Uninstall this application when it falls out of the scope of management

   c. Uninstall this application when no longer needed

   d. none of the above

LAB 12.3 MODIFYING A CUSTOM MSI PACKAGE

Objectives

The goal of this lab is to learn how to use WinINSTALL LE 2003 to modify custom MSI packages.

Materials Required

This lab will require the following:

- A Windows Server 2003 setup, as directed at the front of this lab manual

Estimated completion time: **10 minutes**

Activity Background

While the automatic Discover tool does a good job of creating MSI packages, you may want to modify them. In this activity, you will modify the MSI package you created in Activity 12-1.

 NOTE If the publisher of a software application provides a tool to create transform files (.mst), you should use the tool provided and create a transform rather than edit the MSI package directly. For example, Microsoft Office 2000 and Office XP both have a tool available for creating transform files.

Activity

1. If necessary, start your server and log on using the **Administrator** account in the **CHILDXX** domain (where *XX* is the number of the forest root domain for which your server is a domain controller) using the password **Password01**.

2. Click **Start**, select **All Programs**, and then click **WinINSTALL LE 2003**.

3. In the upper-left tree pane, right-click **Windows Installer Packages** and then click **Import Package**.

4. Click the **...** button.

5. Navigate to **D:\Software\WinZip** (or wherever your software distribution point is if your instructor provided you with an alternate location).

6. Double-click **WinZip.msi**.

7. In the Description text box, enter **WinZip81** (or WinZip*XX*, where *XX* is the version number of WinZip you are using if not 8.1).

8. Check the box next to **Copy Package Source Files**, as shown in Figure 12-5. This will instruct WinINSTALL to import all the support files, not just the .msi file.

Figure 12-5   Importing an existing package

9. Click **OK**.

10. Once the copy process completes, click **OK**.

11. In the upper-left tree pane, confirm that **WinZip81** is selected.

12. In the Version text box, enter **8.1** (or if you downloaded a different version, enter the version number of the version you downloaded).

13. In the Manufacturer text box, enter **WinZip Computing, Inc.**

14. Click the button under **ARP icon**.

15. Click the **...** button.

16. Navigate to **D:\Software\WinZip\Program Files\WinZip** (or wherever your software distribution point is if your instructor provided you with an alternate location).

17. Double-click **WINZIP32.EXE**.

12

18. Select the left-most icon from the Icon list and then click **OK**.

19. Uncheck the check box next to **Show Change button**. Your screen should now look similar to Figure 12-6.

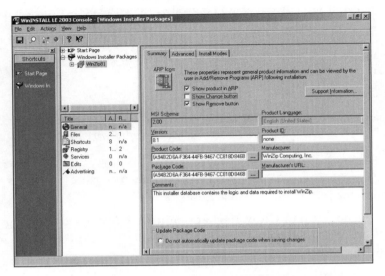

Figure 12-6 Changing Summary options of an MSI package

 NOTE You can also use WinINSTALL to edit the files, shortcuts, registry entries, services, and other items that are installed as part of the MSI package. Doing so is an advanced skill.

20. Click the **File** menu, then click **Save**.

21. Click the **Actions** menu, then click **Compress**.

22. In the Compress dialog box, click **Compress**. This will compress all the extra support files and store them in the .msi file. Once all the support files are stored in the single .msi file, you only need to copy or move the single .msi file as needed.

23. Click **Close**.

24. Close WinINSTALL LE 2003. The MSI package can now be found in C:\Program Files\OnDemand\WinINSTALL\Packages*PACKAGENAME* (Where *PACKAGENAME* is the name of the package).

25. Log off your server if you do not intend to continue immediately to the next project. Otherwise, stay logged on.

Certification Objectives

Objectives for Microsoft Exam #70-294: Planning, Implementing, and Maintaining a Microsoft Windows Server 2003 Active Directory Infrastructure:

- Configure the user environment by using Group Policy

- Deploy a computer environment by using Group Policy

REVIEW QUESTIONS

1. Which of the following actions can be performed in WinINSTALL to store all the extra support files inside the .msi file?

   a. Compile

   b. Compress

   c. Consolidate

   d. Store

2. You can use WinINSTALL to edit which of the following aspects of an MSI package? (Choose all that apply.)

   a. files

   b. registry entries

   c. shortcuts

   d. services

3. When given the option to use a transform file or edit the MSI package directly, it is a better option to use a transform file. True or False?

4. In WinINSTALL, ARP is short for which of the following?

   a. Address Resolution Protocol

   b. Aerospace Recommended Practice

   c. Add or Remove Programs

   d. none of the above

5. Which of the following programs includes a utility to create transform files?

   a. Microsoft Office 2000

   b. Adobe Reader

   c. WinZip

   d. none of the above

12

LAB 12.4 UPGRADING DEPLOYED SOFTWARE

Objectives

The goal of this lab is to learn how to upgrade a package deployed using Group Policy software distribution.

Materials Required

This lab will require the following:

- A Windows Server 2003 setup, as directed at the front of this lab manual

Estimated completion time: **15 minutes**

Activity Background

Software is constantly being patched and updated. Fortunately, Group Policy has built-in features for updating applications that have already been deployed. In this activity, you will upgrade the custom MSI created in Activity 12-1 with the modified MSI created in Activity 12-3. Keep in mind that you can also use these steps when a new version of a software package is available (such as upgrading from version 1.0 to 2.0).

Activity

1. If necessary, start your server and log on using the **Administrator** account in the **CHILDXX** domain (where *XX* is the number of the forest root domain for which your server is a domain controller) using the password **Password01**.

2. Click **Start** and then click **My Computer**.

3. Navigate to **C:\Program Files\OnDemand\WinINSTALL\Packages\ WinZip81** (or WinZip*XX*, where *XX* is the version number of WinZip you are using if not 8.1).

4. Right-click **WinZip.msi** and then click **Copy**.

5. Navigate to **D:\Software**, or the location of your software distribution point if D: is not a hard drive.

6. Click the **Edit** menu, then click **Paste**.

7. Right-click **WinZip.msi** and then click **Rename**. Rename the file to **WinZip81.msi** (or WinZip*XX*.msi, where *XX* is the version number of WinZip you are using if not 8.1). This will make it easier to identify the new package.

8. Close the **Windows Explorer** window.

9. Click **Start**, select **Administrative Tools**, and then click **Active Directory Users and Computers**.

10. If necessary, in the left tree pane, expand the **Domain Controllers organizational unit**.

11. In the left tree pane, right-click the **My Server XX** organizational unit (where *XX* is the number of your server) and then click **Properties**.

12. Click the **Group Policy** tab.

13. Right-click the **My Server XX** GPO link (where *XX* is the number of your server) and then click **Edit** to open the Group Policy Object Editor. Note that if you have installed the GPMC, you will first need to click **Open** to open the GPMC.

14. In the left tree pane, expand **Software Settings** under Computer Configuration.

15. Right-click **Software installation**, select **New**, and then click **Package**.

16. In the File name text box, enter **\\SERVERXX\Software** (where *XX* is the number of your server) and then press **Enter**.

17. Double-click **WinZip81.msi** (or whatever you named the file in Step 7 if you have a different version of WinZip).

18. In the Deploy Software dialog box, select the **Advanced** option and then click **OK**.

19. In the Name text box, enter **WinZip 8.1** (or the appropriate version number, if different).

20. Click the **Deployment** tab.

21. Check the check box next to **Uninstall this application when it falls out of the scope of management**.

22. Click the **Upgrades** tab.

23. Click the **Add** button.

12

24. In the Package to upgrade list box, confirm that **WinZip** is selected, as shown in Figure 12-7.

Figure 12-7   Selecting a package to upgrade

25. Click **OK**. The WinZip package is now listed as being upgraded by the new package.

26. Click **OK**.

27. Close all open windows. If your partner is also performing this lab at the same time, wait for your partner to perform the previous steps before continuing.

NOTE   Because all Group Policy changes are made on the PDC emulator by default, the changes to Group Policy will need to replicate to the other domain controller in your student domain. Before continuing, you should use Active Directory Sites and Services to initiate replication manually from your partner's server.

28. Restart your server. Notice that during the startup process, the messages Removing managed software WinZip and Installing managed software WinZip 8.1 appear.

29. Log on using the **Administrator** account in the **CHILDXX** domain (where *XX* is the number of the forest root domain for which your server is a domain controller) using the password **Password01**.

30. Confirm that WinZip is installed and runs.

31. Log off your server.

Certification Objectives

Objectives for Microsoft Exam #70-294: Planning, Implementing, and Maintaining a Microsoft Windows Server 2003 Active Directory Infrastructure:

■ Maintain installed software by using Group Policy

REVIEW QUESTIONS

1. Which upgrade option requires that all users immediately upgrade to the new version of an application?

    a. Mandatory upgrade

    b. Optional upgrade

    c. Redeployment upgrade

    d. none of the above

2. When you need to deploy a hotfix, it is recommended that you do which of the following?

    a. Create a new package and then perform a mandatory upgrade.

    b. Create a new package and then perform an optional upgrade.

    c. Update the distribution point and then redeploy the existing package.

    d. none of the above

3. The _____ tab is used to specify package upgrade behavior in Group Policy.

4. Both custom .msi files and custom .zap files can be upgraded using Group Policy. True or False?

5. When you perform an optional upgrade on a package assigned to a computer, when is the package upgraded?

    a. when the computer starts

    b. when Group Policy refreshes

    c. when the user manually starts the upgrade in Add or Remove Programs

    d. You cannot perform an optional upgrade on a package assigned to a computer.

12

13

MONITORING AND OPTIMIZING ACTIVE DIRECTORY

Labs included in this chapter:

♦ Lab 13.1 Collecting Baseline Data Using Performance Logs and Alerts

♦ Lab 13.2 Creating Alerts for Active Directory Using Performance Logs and Alerts

♦ Lab 13.3 Reviewing Baseline Data Using Performance Logs and Alerts

♦ Lab 13.4 Changing the Directory Services Restore Mode Password

While all the labs in this chapter pertain to Active Directory, they do not map directly to any MCSE Certification Objectives.

Lab 13.1 Collecting Baseline Data Using Performance Logs and Alerts

Objectives

The goal of this lab is to learn how to collect baseline data related to Active Directory data by using counter logs.

Materials Required

This lab will require the following:

- A Windows Server 2003 setup, as directed at the front of this lab manual

Estimated completion time: **10 minutes**

Activity Background

Many counters in Performance Logs and Alerts do not have a predefined threshold for "good" and "bad" performance. Rather, what constitutes good performance or bad performance for these counters is dependent on the environment and server hardware. In this lab, you will learn how to collect baseline data for comparison to data collected at a later time.

Activity

1. If necessary, start your server and log on using the **Administrator** account in the **CHILDXX** domain (where *XX* is the number of the forest root domain for which your server is a domain controller) using the password **Password01**.

2. Click **Start**, select **Administrative Tools**, and then click **Performance**.

3. In the left tree pane, expand **Performance Logs and Alerts**.

4. In the left tree pane, right-click **Counter Logs** and then click **New Log Settings**.

5. In the Name text box, type **Active Directory Baseline** and then click **OK**.

6. Click **Add Counters**.

7. In the Add Counters dialog box, select **NTDS** from the Performance object drop-down list box.

8. Select the **All counters** option and then click **Add**.

9. Click **Close** to close the Add Counters dialog box.

10. In the Interval spin box, change the value to **30** and ensure that the Units field is set to **seconds**, as shown in Figure 13–1.

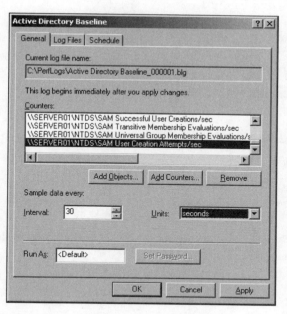

Figure 13-1   Setting interval to collect performance data

11. Click the **Log Files** tab.

12. Ensure that the Log file type is set to **Binary File**.

13. Uncheck the check box next to **End file names with**.

14. Check the check box next to **Overwrite existing log file**.

15. Click the **Schedule** tab.

16. In both the Start log and Stop log areas, select the **Manually** option, if necessary.

17. Click **OK**. If you are prompted that the PerfLogs folder does not exist, click **Yes** to create the folder.

18. If necessary, in the left tree pane, select **Counter Logs** to show a list of logs that have been created in the right details pane.

13

19. In the right details pane, right-click the **Active Directory Baseline** log and then select **Start**. The log icon should appear green to indicate that it is recording data, as shown in Figure 13-2.

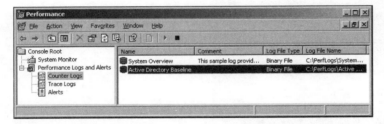

Figure 13-2   Starting a counter log

20. Close the Performance console. You will allow the log to collect data for use in Lab 13–3.

21. Log off your server if you do not intend to continue immediately to the next project. Otherwise, stay logged on.

Certification Objectives

Objectives for Microsoft Exam #70-294: Planning, Implementing, and Maintaining a Microsoft Windows Server 2003 Active Directory Infrastructure:

- Not applicable

REVIEW QUESTIONS

1. Which of the following tools are included in the Performance console? (Choose all that apply.)

   a. System Monitor

   b. Task Manager

   c. Performance Logs and Alerts

   d. Computer Management

2. When selecting a log file type for a counter log, which of the following are valid options? (Choose all that apply.)

   a. a binary file

   b. a comma-delimited text file

   c. a tab-delimited text file

   d. an SQL Database

3. A counter log can be configured to append various combinations of the current date and time to the end of a log file's name. True or False?

4. Counter logs are useful for establishing which of the following?

    a. a maximum for all selected counters

    b. a minimum for all selected counters

    c. a baseline for all selected counters

    d. Counter logs cannot be used to establish any information.

5. You must record every performance object when using counter logs. True or False?

LAB 13.2 CREATING ALERTS FOR ACTIVE DIRECTORY USING PERFORMANCE LOGS AND ALERTS

Objectives

The goal of this lab is to learn how alerts can be set up to notify users when performance counters are above or below a determined threshold.

Materials Required

This lab will require the following:

- A Windows Server 2003 setup, as directed at the front of this lab manual

Estimated completion time: **10 minutes**

13

Activity Background

It is impossible for an administrator to monitor performance data all the time. In order to free administrators from continually watching performance data, alerts can be configured. Alerts can notify an administrator when a counter is above or below a predetermined value. In this lab, you will learn how to create alerts using Performance Logs and Alerts.

NOTE

In order to send and receive alerts, the Messenger service must be started. To start the Messenger service, click Start, select Administrative Tools, and then click Services. In the list of services in the right details pane, right-click the Messenger service and then click Start. You can also have the Messenger service start automatically when the server starts by setting the service's Startup type to automatic in its properties.

Activity

1. If necessary, start your server and log on using the **Administrator** account in the **CHILD XX** domain (where *XX* is the number of the forest root domain for which your server is a domain controller) using the password **Password01**.

2. Click **Start**, select **Administrative Tools**, and then click **Performance**.

3. In the left tree pane, expand **Performance Logs and Alerts**.

4. In the left tree pane, right-click **Alerts** and then click **New Alert Settings**

5. In the Name text box, type **High number of logons** and then click **OK**.

6. Click **Add**.

7. In the Performance object drop-down list box, select **NTDS**.

8. From the list of counters, select the **KDC AS Requests** counter and then click **Add**.

9. Click **Close** to close the Add counters dialog box.

10. In the Alert when the value is drop-down list box, ensure that **Over** is selected.

11. In the Limit text box, enter **10**.

12. In the Interval spin box, ensure that the value is set to **5**.

13. In the Units drop-down list box, select **minutes** as shown in Figure 13-3.

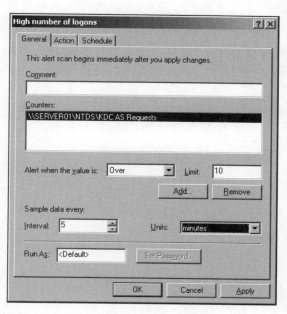

Figure 13-3   Configuring alert criteria

NOTE

If you add multiple counters, any one of the counters can trigger the alert. In other words, only one of the counters must be over or under its limit in order to trigger the alert—not all of the counters.

14. Click the **Action** tab.

15. Uncheck the check box next to **Log an entry in the application event log**.

13

16. Check the box next to **Send a network message to** and enter **SERVERXX** (where *XX* is the number of your server) in the text box, as shown in Figure 13-4.

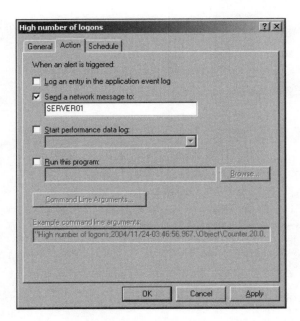

Figure 13-4   Specifying where an alert should be sent

 NOTE   You can enter any valid NetBIOS name to which to send a message, including a user, domain, or computer on the network.

17. Click the **Schedule** tab.

18. In both the Start scan and Stop scan areas, select the **Manually** option, if necessary.

19. Click **OK**.

20. If necessary, in the left tree pane, select **Alerts** to show a list of alerts that have been created in the right details pane.

21. In the right details pane, right-click **High number of logons** and then click start. Every five minutes, the server will check to see if the AS Requests per second are more than 10. If the AS Requests per second are more than 10, an alert message will appear (as a standard Windows message box) on your server.

TIP

If you would like to see what this message looks like, modify the Alert by right-clicking it, selecting Properties, changing the Alert when value is option to **Under**, and then clicking **OK**. This will cause the alert to be sent when less than 10 AS Requests are received per second. You should change the Alert when value is option back to **Over** after viewing the alert. Note that it could take up to five minutes for the alert to appear.

22. Close the Performance console.

23. Log off your server if you do not intend to continue immediately to the next project. Otherwise, stay logged on.

Certification Objectives

Objectives for Microsoft Exam #70-294: Planning, Implementing, and Maintaining a Microsoft Windows Server 2003 Active Directory Infrastructure:

■ Not applicable

REVIEW QUESTIONS

1. Which of the following are not actions associated with an alert?

   a. Send a network message to

   b. Start performance data log

   c. Run this program

   d. Disable a service

2. Which type of NetBIOS names can alerts be sent to?

   a. users

   b. computers

   c. domains

   d. all of the above

3. Unlike logs, alerts are always running and cannot be started or stopped. True or False?

13

4. When an alert occurs, an event can be added to which of the following logs?

   a. the System event log

   b. the Security event log

   c. the Application event log

   d. It depends what counter caused the alert.

5. In order for an alert with multiple counters to be triggered, all counters must be over or under (whichever is selected) their specified limits. True or False?

LAB 13.3 REVIEWING BASELINE DATA USING PERFORMANCE LOGS AND ALERTS

Objectives

The goal of this lab is to learn how a counter log can be viewed using the Performance console.

Materials Required

This lab will require the following:

- A Windows Server 2003 setup, as directed at the front of this lab manual

Estimated completion time: **10 minutes**

Activity Background

Viewing previously recorded data is useful when you need to compare baseline data to current activity. Comparing previous performance to current performance can help you identify and diagnose problems. In this lab, you will learn how to use Performance Logs and Alerts to view the log you started recording in Lab 13-1.

ACTIVITY

Activity

1. If necessary, start your server and log on using the **Administrator** account in the **CHILDXX** domain (where *XX* is the number of the forest root domain for which your server is a domain controller) using the password **Password01**.

2. Click **Start**, select **Administrative Tools**, and then click **Performance**.

3. In the left tree pane, expand **Performance Logs and Alerts**.

4. In the left tree pane, select **Counter Logs** to show a list of logs that have been created in the right details pane.

5. In the right details pane, right-click the **Active Directory Baseline** log and then select **Stop**. This will end recording of performance data.

6. In the left tree pane, select **System Monitor**.

7. In the right details pane, click the **New Counter Set** toolbar item.

8. In the right details pane, click the **View Log Data** toolbar item. (It looks like a gray database icon.)

9. In the Data source area, select the **Log files** option.

10. Click **Add**.

11. Navigate to the **C:\perflogs** folder and then double-click the **Active Directory Baseline.blg** file to open the log. The log you created should now be listed as the only data source, as shown in Figure 13-5.

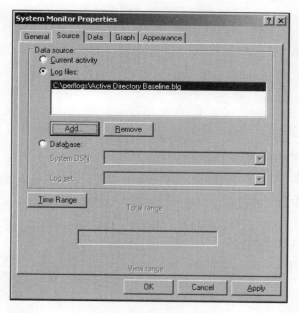

Figure 13-5   Selecting an existing counter log as the data source

12. Click the **Time Range** button. The upper set of dates and times indicates the start and endpoints of the log. The lower set of dates and times indicates the range of data that is actually shown on the graph. You can use the left- and right-most parts of the slider to adjust the displayed date and time range.

13. Click the **Data** tab.

14. Click **Add**.

15. From the list of counters, select **DS Directory Reads/sec** and then click **Add**.

16. From the list of counters, select **DS Directory Writes/sec** and then click **Add**.

17. Click **Close** to close the Add Counters dialog box.

18. Click the **Graph** tab.

19. In the Vertical scale area, type **5** in the Maximum text box. Changing the vertical scale can make it easier to view small variations in performance data. Note that in a production environment, you will probably set this value much higher. However, in your test environment, not many read or write operations will occur, so the graph must be modified so you can see the activity.

20. Click **OK**. Your console should now look similar to Figure 13-6.

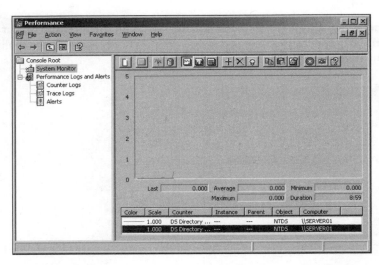

Figure 13-6   Viewing performance data from a counter log

21. Close the Performance console.

22. Log off your server if you do not intend to continue immediately to the next project. Otherwise, stay logged on.

Certification Objectives

Objectives for Microsoft Exam #70-294: Planning, Implementing, and Maintaining a Microsoft Windows Server 2003 Active Directory Infrastructure:

- Not applicable

REVIEW QUESTIONS

1. Which of the following are valid sources for performance data? (Choose all that apply.)

   a. current activity

   b. log files

   c. a database

   d. none of the above

2. When viewing a counter log, an administrator can specify the date and time range within the log they would like to view. True or False?

3. Changing which of the following options can make it easier to view small variations in performance data?

   a. Vertical scale

   b. Vertical grid

   c. Horizontal scale

   d. none of the above

4. Which of the following views is enabled when viewing data from a log file?

   a. Graph

   b. Histogram

   c. Report

   d. all of the above

5. You do not have to display every counter that is recorded by a log. True or False?

LAB 13.4 CHANGING THE DIRECTORY SERVICES RESTORE MODE PASSWORD

Objectives

The goal of this lab is to learn how the Directory Services Restore Mode password can be changed using Ntdsutil.

Materials Required

This lab will require the following:

- A Windows Server 2003 setup, as directed at the front of this lab manual

Estimated completion time: **5 minutes**

Activity Background

When a domain controller starts in normal mode, it can use Active Directory to authenticate users. However, when a domain controller starts in Directory Services Restore Mode, Active Directory is offline. In order for the administrator to log on to the server, the domain controller uses a local SAM database containing an account called Administrator. The administrator can then use the Administrator account in the local SAM database to log on to the workstation.

While the domain controller's local SAM database is not used in normal mode, you can use Ntdsutil to change the Directory Services Restore Mode password. Changing the Directory Services Restore Mode password changes the password for the Administrator account in the local SAM database. In this lab, you will learn how to change the Directory Services Restore Mode password using Ntdsutil.

Activity

1. If necessary, start your server and log on using the **Administrator** account in the **CHILDXX** domain (where *XX* is the number of the forest root domain for which your server is a domain controller) using the password **Password01**.

2. Click **Start** and then click **Command Prompt**.

3. Type **Ntdsutil** and then press **Enter**.

4. At the Ntdsutil prompt, type **Set DSRM Password** and then press **Enter**.

5. At the **Reset DSRM Administrator Password** prompt, type **Reset Password on server SERVERXX** (where *XX* is the number of your server) and then press **Enter**. (Note that you could also substitute *localhost* instead of the name of your server to change the Directory Services Restore Mode password on the server where Ntdsutil is being run.)

6. Type **DSRM01** and then press **Enter**.

7. Type **DSRM01** again to confirm the new password and then press **Enter**. A message will inform you if the password was successfully reset or not, as shown in Figure 13-7.

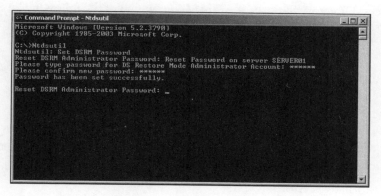

Figure 13-7   Resetting the Directory Services Restore Mode password

8. You will now change the password back to what it originally was: Password01. At the **Reset DSRM Administrator Password** prompt, type **Reset Password on server localhost** and then press **Enter**.

9. Type **Password01** and then press **Enter**.

10. Type **Password01** again to confirm the password and then press **Enter**.

11. Type **Quit** and then press **Enter** to return to the Ntdsutil prompt.

12. Type **Quit** to exit the Ntdsutil utility.

13. Close the command prompt window.

14. Log off your server.

Certification Objectives

Objectives for Microsoft Exam #70-294: Planning, Implementing, and Maintaining a Microsoft Windows Server 2003 Active Directory Infrastructure:

- Not applicable

13

REVIEW QUESTIONS

1. To access Directory Services Restore Mode, which of the following keys should you press at startup?

    a. F4

    b. F6

    c. F8

    d. F10

2. Which of the following actions require that a domain controller be restarted in Directory Services Restore Mode? (Choose all that apply.)

    a. Authoritative restore

    b. Non–authoritative restore

    c. Integrity check

    d. Semantic check

3. You can use the _____ command-line utility to reset the Directory Services Restore Mode password.

4. When is the Directory Services Restore Mode password initially set?

    a. when Windows is installed

    b. during the promotion process

    c. the first time Directory Services Restore Mode is used

    d. the first time Ntdsutil is used

5. The Directory Services Restore Mode password is the same on all domain controllers in a domain. True or False?

14

DISASTER RECOVERY

Labs included in this chapter:

♦ Lab 14.1 Testing a Backup Type's Effect on System State Backups

♦ Lab 14.2 Scheduling System State Backups

♦ Lab 14.3 Using NETDOM to Reset a Trust Relationship

♦ Lab 14.4 Using NETDOM to Verify a Trust Relationship

Microsoft MCSE Exam #70-294 Objectives	
Objective	Lab
Implement an Active Directory directory service forest and domain structure.	14.4
Manage an Active Directory forest and domain structure.	14.3, 14.4

LAB 14.1 TESTING A BACKUP TYPE'S EFFECT ON SYSTEM STATE BACKUPS

Objectives

The goal of this lab is to demonstrate that the System State portion of a backup is always backed up using the normal method, regardless of which backup type is selected.

Materials Required

This lab will require the following:

- A Windows Server 2003 setup, as directed at the front of this lab manual

- A normal backup of the System State called systemstate.bkf, located on the D: drive. (If you have completed the activities in the main text associated with this lab manual, this backup should already exist.) Note that if D: is not a hard drive, you will need to substitute D: for the drive letter that holds the systemstate.bkf file in this lab

Estimated completion time: **15 minutes**

Activity Background

While the Windows Server 2003 Backup Utility lets you make a normal backup, a differential backup, and an incremental backup of files and folders, the System State is always backed up using a normal backup—even if you select a different backup type. This means that all files and folders that make up the System State are backed up—even if they have not changed from the last backup that was made. In this lab, you will test this behavior by comparing the size of a System State backup when the normal backup type is selected and when the incremental backup type is selected.

Activity

1. If necessary, start your server and log on using the **Administrator** account in the **CHILDXX** domain (where *XX* is the number of the forest root domain for which your server is a domain controller) using the password **Password01**.

2. Click **Start**, select **All Programs**, select **Accessories**, select **System Tools**, and then click **Backup**.

3. If the Backup or Restore Wizard appears, click the **Advanced Mode** link to open the Backup Utility window. Otherwise, continue with the next step.

4. Click the **Backup** tab.

5. In the left tree pane, check the check box next to **System State**.

6. In the Backup media or file name text box, enter **D:\incrementaltest.bkf**, as shown in Figure 14-1. Note that your instructor may provide you with an alternate location if you do not have a hard drive labeled D:.

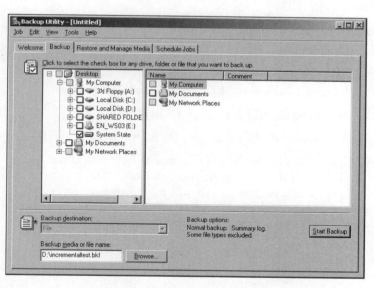

Figure 14-1   Backing up the System State data

7. Click **Start Backup**.

8. Click the **Advanced** button.

9. In the Backup Type drop-down list box, select **Incremental**, as shown in Figure 14-2.

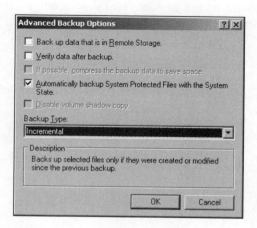

Figure 14-2   Selecting the backup type

10. Click **OK**.

14

11. Click **Start Backup**.

12. When the backup completes, click **Close**.

13. Close the Backup Utility.

14. Click **Start** and then click **My Computer**.

15. Double-click the **D:** drive or the drive that contains incrementaltest.bkf if D: is not a hard drive.

16. Right-click **incrementaltest.bkf** and then click **Properties**.

17. Note the size of the file and then click **Cancel**.

18. Right-click **systemstate.bkf** and then click **Properties**.

19. Note the size of the file. While the systemstate.bkf backup was made using the normal backup type and the incrementaltest.bkf backup was made using the incremental backup type, the files should be approximately the same size. This shows that regardless of the backup type selected, the System State portion of a backup is always backed up using the normal backup type.

NOTE   Keep in mind that this behavior is only for the System State portion of a backup. If you back up more than just the System State, all other files will use the backup type you select, while the System State portion will use a normal backup. For example, if you back up the C: drive plus the System State using the incremental backup type, the System State will use the normal backup method, while the C: drive would be backed up using the incremental backup method.

20. Click **Cancel**.

21. Close the Windows Explorer window.

22. Log off your server if you do not intend to continue immediately to the next project. Otherwise, stay logged on.

Certification Objectives

Objectives for Microsoft Exam #70-294: Planning, Implementing, and Maintaining a Microsoft Windows Server 2003 Active Directory Infrastructure:

■ Not applicable

REVIEW QUESTIONS

1. A System State backup is always backed up using which of the following methods?

    a. normal

    b. differential

    c. incremental

    d. It depends on the backup type selected.

2. If you back up both the C: drive and the System State in the same backup, choosing the differential backup type, which of the following methods would be used to back up the data?

    a. The C: drive would be backed up using the normal backup method and the System State would be backed up using the normal backup method.

    b. The C: drive would be backed up using the normal backup method and the System State would be backed up using the differential backup method.

    c. The C: drive would be backed up using the differential backup method and the System State would be backed up using the normal backup method.

    d. The C: drive would be backed up using the differential backup method and the System State would be backed up using the differential backup method.

3. Which of the following is not backed up as part of the System State?

    a. Registry

    b. Certificate Services database

    c. Active Directory

    d. Program Files folder

4. If resources are available only to back up one domain controller per domain, which of the following domain controllers would be the best choice to back up?

    a. a domain controller holding no operations master roles

    b. the domain controller holding the PDC emulator role

    c. the domain controller holding the RID master role

    d. the domain controller holding the Infrastructure master role

14

5. Which of the following is not backed up as part of the System State?

   a. boot files

   b. system files

   c. user files

   d. SYSVOL directory

LAB 14.2 SCHEDULING SYSTEM STATE BACKUPS

Objectives

The goal of this lab is to learn how to schedule System State backups using the Windows Server 2003 Backup Utility.

Materials Required

This lab will require the following:

- A Windows Server 2003 setup, as directed at the front of this lab manual

Estimated completion time: **10 minutes**

Activity Background

Backups of Active Directory should be made on a regular basis. To ensure that backups are made on a regular schedule, the Backup Utility can be used to schedule backups that occur automatically. In this lab, you will learn how to schedule backups of the System State data using the Backup Utility.

Activity

1. If necessary, start your server and log on using the **Administrator** account in the **CHILDXX** domain (where *XX* is the number of the forest root domain for which your server is a domain controller) using the password **Password01**.

2. Click **Start**, select **All Programs**, select **Accessories**, select **System Tools**, and then click **Backup**.

3. If the Backup or Restore Wizard appears, click the **Advanced Mode** link to open the Backup Utility window. Otherwise, continue with the next step.

4. Click the **Schedule Jobs** tab.

5. Click **Add Job**.

6. Click **Next** on the Welcome to the Backup Wizard window.

7. In the What to Back Up window, select the **Only back up the System State data** option, as shown in Figure 14–3.

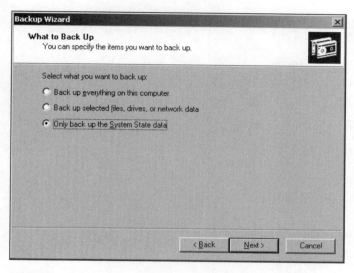

Figure 14-3   Selecting what to back up

8. Click **Next**.

9. In the Backup Type, Destination, and Name window, click **Browse**.

10. If necessary, navigate to the D: drive using the Save in drop-down list. Note that your instructor may provide you with an alternate location if you do not have a hard drive labeled D:.

11. In the File name drop-down combo box, type **SunSysStat** and then click **Save**.

12. Click **Next**.

13. On the How to Back Up window, leave the default options and then click **Next**.

14. On the Backup Options window, select the **Replace the existing backups** option to overwrite the backup if it already exists.

15. Click **Next**.

16. On the When to Back Up window, ensure that the **Later** option is selected and then enter **Sunday System State backup** in the Job name text box.

17. Click **Set Schedule**.

18. In the Schedule Task drop-down list, select **Weekly**.

19. In the Start time spin box, set the time to **9:00 PM**.

20. Ensure that the Every spin box is set to **1**.

21. Uncheck the box next to **Mon**.

14

22. Check the check box next to **Sun**, as shown in Figure 14-4. This schedule will perform a backup of the System State every Sunday.

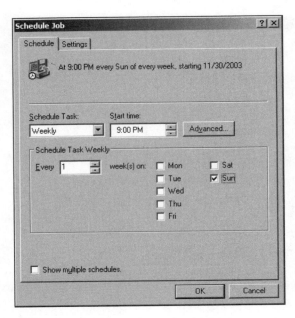

Figure 14-4   Scheduling a backup job

23. Click **OK**.

24. You will then be prompted for credentials to be used when running the backup. In the Password and Confirm password text boxes, enter **Password01**.

TIP

In a production environment, creating a user account dedicated to scheduled tasks, such as backups, can make management simpler.

25. Click **OK**.

26. Click **Next**.

27. If you are prompted for credentials again, enter **Password01** in the Password and Confirm password text boxes and then click **OK**.

28. Click **Finish** to close the wizard and create the scheduled backup. You should now notice that the calendar on the **Schedule Jobs** tab has a small backup icon on every Sunday after the present day (advance to the next month, if necessary). You can click the icon to view details on the backup job or to delete the backup job altogether.

29. Close the Backup Utility.

30. Log off your server if you do not intend to continue immediately to the next project. Otherwise, stay logged on.

Certification Objectives

Objectives for Microsoft Exam #70-294: Planning, Implementing, and Maintaining a Microsoft Windows Server 2003 Active Directory Infrastructure:

- Not applicable

REVIEW QUESTIONS

1. The Backup utility included with Windows Server 2003 allows backup jobs to be scheduled. True or False?

2. In most cases, you should back up Active Directory how often?

   a. once an hour

   b. once a day

   c. once a week

   d. once every 60 days

3. Which of the following are benefits of storing backups on removable media? (Choose all that apply.)

   a. offsite storage

   b. fast access to data at all times

   c. do not need to be stored securely

   d. not susceptible to viruses once removed from the network

4. In a production environment, creating a user account dedicated to scheduled tasks, such as backups, can make management simpler. True or False?

5. A disaster recovery plan should include which of the following? (Choose all that apply.)

   a. a description of how often backups are made

   b. a description of where backups are stored

   c. server hardware specifications

   d. a list of people who should be contacted in the event of a disaster

14

Lab 14.3 Using NETDOM to Reset a Trust Relationship

Objectives

The goal of this lab is to learn how to use the NETDOM utility included with the Windows Server 2003 support tools to reset a trust relationship.

Only one member of each student group should perform these steps at a time. If your partner has already started, wait for him or her to finish before continuing.

Materials Required

This lab will require the following:

- A Windows Server 2003 setup, as directed at the front of this lab manual

Estimated completion time: **5 minutes**

Activity Background

A trust relationship is based on a password that is only known by the trusted and trusting domains. For security reasons, a new password is chosen every seven days and the previous password is also stored (in case a crash occurs just after the passwords are changed on one end). In other words, this means that a trust password is valid for up to 14 days. If one of the domains is authoritatively restored from a backup that is older than 14 days, the passwords used by the trusted and trusting domains will become out of sync. In order to set the password to one that is known by both domains, the trust must be reset. You will learn how to reset trust relationships using NETDOM in this lab.

Activity

1. If necessary, start your server and log on using the **Administrator** account in the **CHILDXX** domain (where *XX* is the number of the forest root domain for which your server is a domain controller) using the password **Password01**.

2. Click **Start** and then click **Command Prompt**.

3. Type **NETDOM TRUST CHILD*XX* /D:SUPERCORP /UD:Administrator /PD:Password01 /Reset /Twoway /Verbose** (where *XX* is the number of the forest root domain for which your server is a domain controller) and then press **Enter**. If the trust is reset successfully, the output displayed should look similar to Figure 14–5.

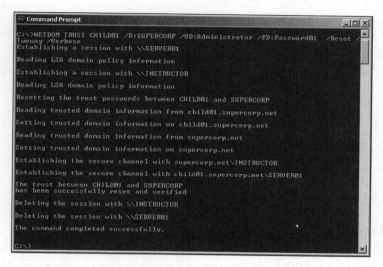

Figure 14-5   Resetting a trust relationship using NETDOM

NOTE

If the trust relationship is not reset successfully, ensure that the instructor server is up and running. Also confirm that your server is able to resolve and communicate with the instructor server by entering PING INSTRUCTOR.supercorp.net at a command prompt.

4. Close the command prompt window.

5. Log off your server if you do not intend to continue immediately to the next project. Otherwise, stay logged on.

TIP

For more details on the NETDOM TRUST syntax, you can type NETDOM TRUST /? at a command prompt.

Certification Objectives

Objectives for Microsoft Exam #70-294: Planning, Implementing, and Maintaining a Microsoft Windows Server 2003 Active Directory Infrastructure:

■ Manage an Active Directory forest and domain structure.

14

REVIEW QUESTIONS

1. Use the _____ parameter of the NETDOM TRUST command to specify the name of the trusted domain.

2. Use the _____ parameter of the NETDOM TRUST command when the password for a trust becomes out of sync between two domains. That is, this parameter will set the password to be the same in both domains for the trust.

3. Which of the following actions may require that a trust (or trusts) be reset?

   a. a non-authoritative restore

   b. an authoritative restore

   c. soft recovery

   d. semantic check

4. Use the _____ parameter of the NETDOM TRUST command to specify the account used to make the connection with the domain specified by the /Domain (or /D) argument.

5. Specifying which of the following characters as the password tells NETDOM to prompt you for the password?

   a. exclamation point (!)

   b. question mark (?)

   c. asterisk (*)

   d. ampersand (&)

LAB 14.4 USING NETDOM TO VERIFY A TRUST RELATIONSHIP

Objectives

The goal of this lab is to learn how to use the NETDOM utility included with the Windows Server 2003 support tools to verify a trust relationship.

Materials Required

This lab will require the following:

■ A Windows Server 2003 setup, as directed at the front of this lab manual